The Authorship of the Fourth Gospel:

EXTERNAL EVIDENCES.

EZRA ABBOT, D.D., LL.D.,

*Bussey Professor of New Testament Criticism and Interpretation
in the Divinity School of Harvard University*

Wipf and Stock Publishers
150 West Broadway • Eugene OR 97401
2000

The Authorship of the Fourth Gospel

By Abbott, Ezra

ISBN: 1-57910-515-7

Reprinted by *Wipf and Stock Publishers*
150 West Broadway • Eugene OR 97401

Previously published by Geo H. Ellis, 1880.

PREFATORY NOTE.

THE following essay was read, in part, before the "Ministers' Institute," at its public meeting last October, in Providence, R.I. In considering the external evidences of the genuineness of the Gospel ascribed to John, it was out of the question, under the circumstances, to undertake anything more than the discussion of a few important points; and even these could not be properly treated within the time allowed.

In revising the paper for the *Unitarian Review* (February, March, June, 1880), and, with additions and corrections, for the volume of "Institute Essays," I have greatly enlarged some parts of it, particularly that relating to the evidence that the Fourth Gospel was used by Justin Martyr. The consideration of his quotations and of the hypotheses connected with them has given occasion to the long Notes appended to the essay, in which will be found the results of some original investigation. But the circumstances under which the essay is printed have compelled me to treat other parts of the evidence for the genuineness of this Gospel less thoroughly than I wished, and on certain points to content myself with mere references. It has also been necessary to give in a translation many quotations which scholars would have preferred to see in the original; but the translation has been made as literal as the English idiom would permit, and precise references to the passages cited are always given for the benefit of the critical student.

E. A.

CAMBRIDGE, MASS., May 21, 1880.

THE AUTHORSHIP OF THE FOURTH GOSPEL:

EXTERNAL EVIDENCES.

THE problem of the Fourth Gospel — that is, the question of its authorship and historical value — requires for its complete solution a consideration of many collateral questions which are still in debate. Until these are gradually disposed of by thorough investigation and discussion, we can hardly hope for a general agreement on the main question at issue. Such an agreement among scholars certainly does not at present exist. Since the "epoch-making" essay (to borrow a favorite phrase of the Germans) of Ferdinand Christian Baur, in the *Theologische Jahrbücher* for 1844, there has indeed been much shifting of ground on the part of the opponents of the genuineness of the Gospel; but among scholars of equal learning and ability, as Hilgenfeld, Keim, Scholten, Hausrath, Renan, on the one hand, and Godet, Beyschlag, Luthardt, Weiss, Lightfoot, on the other, opinions are yet divided, with a tendency, at least in Germany, toward the denial of its genuineness. Still, some of these collateral questions of which I have spoken seem to be approaching a settlement. I may notice first one of the most important, the question whether the relation of the Apostle John to Jewish Christianity was not such that it is impossible to suppose the Fourth Gospel to have proceeded from him, even at a late period of his life. This is a fundamental postulate of the theory of the Tübingen School, in regard to the opposition of Paul to the three great Apostles, Peter, James, and John. The Apostle John, they say, wrote the Apocalypse, the most Jewish of all the books of the New Testament; but he could not have written the anti-Judaic Gospel. Recognizing most fully the great service which Baur and his followers have rendered to the history of primitive Christianity by their bold and searching investigations, I think it may be said that there is a wide-spread and deepening conviction among fair-minded scholars that the theory of the Tübingen School, in the form in which it has been presented by the coryphæi of the party, as Baur, Schwegler, Zeller, is an extreme view, resting largely on a false interpretation of many passages of the New Testament, and a false view of many early Christian writings. Matthew Arnold's protest against the excessive "vigour and rigour" of the Tübingen theories brings a good deal of plain English common-sense to bear on the subject, and exposes well some of the extravagances of Baur and others.* Still more weight is to be attached to the emphatic dissent of such an able and thoroughly independent scholar as Dr. James Donaldson, the author of the *Critical History of Christian Literature and Doctrine*, a work unhappily unfinished. But very significant is the remarkable article of Keim on the Apostolic Council at Jerusalem, in his latest work, *Aus dem Urchristenthum* ("Studies in the History of Early Christianity"), published in 1878, a short time before his lamented death. In this able essay, he demolishes the foundation of the Tübingen theory, vindicating in the main the historical character of the account in the Acts, and exposing the misinterpretation of the passage in the Epistle to the Galatians, on which Baur and his followers found their view of the absolute contradiction between the Acts and the Epistle. Holtzmann, Lipsius, Pfleiderer, and especially Weizsäcker had already gone far in modifying the extreme view of Baur; but this essay of Keim's is a re-examination of the whole question with reference to all the recent discussions. The still later work of Schenkel,

---

* See his *God and the Bible*, Preface, and chaps. v., vi.

published during the present year (1879), *Das Christusbild der Apostel und der nachapostolischen Zeit* ("The Picture of Christ presented by the Apostles and by the Post-Apostolic Time"), is another conspicuous example of the same reaction. Schenkel remarks in the Preface to this volume: —

> Having never been able to convince myself of the sheer opposition between Petrinism and Paulinism, it has also never been possible for me to get a credible conception of a reconciliation effected by means of a literature sailing between the contending parties under false colors. In respect to the Acts of the Apostles, in particular, I have been led in part to different results from those represented by the modern critical school. I have been forced to the conviction that it is a far more trustworthy source of information than is commonly allowed on the part of the modern criticism; that older documents worthy of credit, besides the well-known *We*-source, are contained in it; and that the Paulinist who composed it has not intentionally distorted (*entstellt*) the facts, but only placed them in the light in which they appeared to him and must have appeared to him from the time and circumstances under which he wrote. He has not, in my opinion, artificially brought upon the stage either a Paulinized Peter, or a Petrinized Paul, in order to mislead his readers, but has portrayed the two apostles just as he actually conceived of them on the basis of his incomplete information. (Preface, pp. x., xi.)

It would be hard to find two writers more thoroughly independent, whatever else may be said of them, than Keim and Schenkel. Considering their well-known position, they will hardly be stigmatized as "apologists" in the contemptuous sense in which that term is used by some recent writers, who seem to imagine that they display their freedom from partisan bias by giving their opponents bad names. On this subject of the one-sidedness of the Tübingen School, I might also refer to the very valuable remarks of Professor Fisher in his recent work on *The Beginnings of Christianity*, and in his earlier volume on *The Supernatural Origin of Christianity*. One of the ablest discussions of the question will also be found in the Essay on "St. Paul and the Three," appended to the commentary on the Epistle to the Galatians, by Professor Lightfoot, now Bishop of Durham, a scholar who has no superior among the Germans in breadth of learning and thoroughness of research. The dissertation of Professor

Jowett on "St. Paul and the Twelve," though not very definite in its conclusions, likewise deserves perusal.*

In regard to this collateral question, then, I conceive that decided progress has been made in a direction favorable to the possibility (to put it mildly) of the Johannean authorship of the Fourth Gospel. We do not know anything concerning the theological position of the Apostle John, which justifies us in assuming that twenty years after the destruction of Jerusalem he could not have written such a work.

Another of these collateral questions, on which a vast amount has been written, and on which very confident and very untenable assertions have been made, may now, I believe, be regarded as set at rest, so far as concerns our present subject, the authorship of the Fourth Gospel. I refer to the history of the Paschal controversies of the second century. The thorough discussion of this subject by Schürer, formerly Professor Extraordinarius at Leipzig, and now Professor at Giessen, the editor of the *Theologische Literaturzeitung*, and author of the excellent *Neutestamentliche Zeitgeschichte*, has clearly shown, I believe, that no argument against the Johannean authorship of the Fourth Gospel can be drawn from the entangled history of these controversies. His essay, in which the whole previous literature of the subject is carefully reviewed, and all the original sources critically examined, was published in Latin at Leipzig in 1869 under the title *De Controversiis Paschalibus secundo post Christum natum Saeculo exortis*, and afterwards in a German translation in Kahnis's *Zeitschrift für die historische Theologie* for 1870, pp. 182–284. There is, according to him, absolutely *no* evidence that the Apostle John celebrated Easter with the Quartodecimans on the 14th of Nisan in commemoration, as is so often assumed, of the day of the *Lord's Supper*. The choice of the day had no reference

---

* In his work on *The Epistles of St. Paul to the Thessalonians, Galatians, Romans*, 2d ed. (London, 1859), i. 417–477; reprinted in a less complete form from the first edition in Noyes's *Theol. Essays* (1856), p. 357 ff. The very judicious remarks of Mr. Norton on the difference between Paul and the other Apostles, and between the Jewish and Gentile Christians, in his article on the "Authorship of the Epistle to the Hebrews," in the *Christian Examiner* for May, 1829, vol. vi. p. 200 ff., are still worth reading.

to that event, nor on the other hand, as Weitzel and Steitz maintain, to the supposed day of Christ's death, but was determined by the fact that the 14th was the day of the Jewish Passover, for which the Christian festival was substituted. The celebration was Christian, but the *day* adopted by John and the Christians of Asia Minor generally was the *day* of the Jewish Passover, the 14th of Nisan, on whatever day of the week it might fall, while the Western Christians generally, without regard to the day of the month, celebrated Easter on Sunday, in commemoration of the day of the resurrection. This is the view essentially of Lücke, Gieseler, Bleek, De Wette, Hase, and Riggenbach, with differences on subordinate points; but Schürer has made the case clearer than any other writer. Schürer is remarkable among German scholars for a calm, judicial spirit, and for thoroughness of investigation; and his judgment in this matter is the more worthy of regard, as he does not receive the Gospel of John as genuine. A good exposition of the subject, founded on Schürer's discussion, may be found in Luthardt's work on the *Authorship of the Fourth Gospel*, of which an English translation has been published, with an Appendix by Dr. Gregory of Leipzig, giving the literature of the whole controversy on the authorship of the Gospel far more completely than it has ever before been presented.

Another point may be mentioned, as to which there has come to be a general agreement; namely, that the very late date assigned to the Gospel by Baur and Schwegler, namely, somewhere between the years 160 and 170 A.D., cannot be maintained. Zeller and Scholten retreat to 150; Hilgenfeld, who is at last constrained to admit its use by Justin Martyr, goes back to between 130 and 140; Renan now says 125 or 130; Keim in the first volume of his *History of Jesus of Nazara* placed it with great confidence between the years 110 and 115, or more loosely, A.D. 100–117.* The fatal consequences of such an admission as that were, however, soon perceived; and in the last volume of his *History*

---

* *Geschichte Jesu von Nazara*, i. 155, comp. 146 (Eng. trans. i. 211, comp. 199).

of Jesus, and in the last edition of his abridgment of that work, he goes back to the year 130.* Schenkel assigns it to A.D. 115–120. †

This enforced shifting of the date of the Gospel to the earlier part of the second century (which I may remark incidentally is fatal to the theory that its author borrowed from Justin Martyr instead of Justin from John) at once presents very serious difficulties on the supposition of the spuriousness of the Gospel. It is the uniform tradition, supported by great weight of testimony, that the Evangelist John lived to a very advanced age, spending the latter portion of his life in Asia Minor, and dying there in the reign of Trajan, not far from A.D. 100. How could a spurious Gospel of a character so peculiar, so different from the earlier Synoptic Gospels, so utterly unhistorical as it is affirmed to be, gain currency as the work of the Apostle both among Christians and the Gnostic heretics, if it originated only twenty-five or thirty years after his death, when so many who must have known whether he wrote such a work or not were still living?

The feeling of this difficulty seems to have revived the theory, put forward, to be sure, as long ago as 1840 by a very wild German writer, Lützelberger, but which Baur and Strauss deemed unworthy of notice, that the Apostle John was never in Asia Minor at all. This view has recently found strenuous advocates in Keim, Scholten, and others, though it is rejected and, I believe, fully refuted by critics of the same school, as Hilgenfeld. The historical evidence against it seems to me decisive; and to attempt to support it, as Scholten does, by purely arbitrary conjectures, such as the denial of the genuineness of the letter of Irenæus to Florinus, can only give one the impression that the writer has a desperate cause.‡

---

* *Geschichte Jesu . . . für weitere Kreise*, 3ᵉ Bearbeitung, 2ᵉ Aufl. (1875), p. 40.

† *Das Charakterbild Jesu*, 4ᵉ Aufl. (1873), p. 370.

‡ See Hilgenfeld, *Hist. Krit. Einleitung in d. N. T.* (1875), p. 394 ff.; Bleek, *Einl. in d. N. T.*, 3ᵉ Aufl. (1875), p. 167 ff., with Mangold's note; Fisher, *The Beginnings of Christianity* (1877), p. 327 ff. Compare Renan, *L'Antechrist*, p. 557 ff.

Thus far we have noticed a few points connected with the controversy about the authorship of the Fourth Gospel in respect to which some progress may seem to have been made since the time of Baur. Others will be remarked upon incidentally, as we proceed. But to survey the whole field of discussion in an hour's discourse is impossible. To treat the question of the historical evidence with any thoroughness would require a volume; to discuss the internal character of the Gospel in its bearings on the question of its genuineness and historical value would require a much larger one. All therefore which I shall now attempt will be to consider some points of the historical evidence for the genuineness of the Fourth Gospel, as follows:—

1. The general reception of the Four Gospels as genuine among Christians in the last quarter of the second century.

2. The question respecting the inclusion of the Fourth Gospel in the Apostolical Memoirs of Christ appealed to by Justin Martyr.

3. Its use by the various Gnostic sects.

4. The attestation to this Gospel which has come down to us appended to the book itself.

I begin with the statement, which cannot be questioned, that our present four Gospels, and no others, were received by the great body of Christians as genuine and sacred books during the last quarter of the second century. This appears most clearly from the writings of Irenæus, born not far from A.D. 125–130, whose youth was spent in Asia Minor, and who became Bishop of Lyons in Gaul, A.D. 178; of Clement, the head of the Catechetical School at Alexandria about the year 190, who had travelled in Greece, Italy, Syria, and Palestine, seeking religious instruction; and of Tertullian, in North Africa, who flourished toward the close of the century. The four Gospels are found in the ancient Syriac version of the New Testament, the Peshito, made in the second century, the authority of which has the more weight as it omits the Second and Third Epistles of John, Second Peter, Jude, and the Apocalypse, books whose authorship was disputed in the early Church. Their existence in the Old Latin version also attests their currency in North Africa, where that version originated some time in the second century. They appear, moreover, in the Muratorian Canon, written probably about A.D. 170, the oldest list of canonical books which has come down to us.

Mr. Norton in his work on the *Genuineness of the Gospels* argues with great force that, when we take into consideration the peculiar character of the Gospels, and the character and circumstances of the community by which they were received, the fact of their universal reception at this period admits of no reasonable explanation except on the supposition that they are genuine. I do not here contend for so broad an inference: I only maintain that this fact proves that our four Gospels could not have originated at this period, but must have been in existence long before; and that some very powerful influence must have been at work to effect their universal reception. I shall not recapitulate Mr. Norton's arguments; but I would call attention to one point on which he justly lays great stress, though it is often overlooked; namely, that the main evidence for the genuineness of the Gospels is of an altogether different kind from that which can be adduced for the genuineness of any classical work. It is not the testimony of a few eminent Christian writers to their private opinion, but it is the evidence which they afford of the belief of the whole body of Christians; and this, not in respect to ordinary books, whose titles they might easily take on trust, but respecting books in which they were most deeply interested; books which were the very foundation of that faith which separated them from the world around them, exposed them to hatred, scorn, and persecution, and often demanded the sacrifice of life itself.

I would add that the greater the differences between the Gospels, real or apparent, the more difficult it must have been for them to gain this universal reception, except on the supposition that they had been handed down from the beginning as genuine. This remark applies particularly to the Fourth Gospel when compared with the first three.

The remains of Christian literature in the first three quarters of the second century are scanty, and are of such a character that, assuming the genuineness of the Gospels, we have really no reason to expect more definite references to their writers, and more numerous quotations from or allusions to them than we actually do find or seem to find. A few letters, as the Epistle of Clement of Rome to the Corinthians, now made complete by the discovery of a new MS. and of a Syriac version of it; the Epistle ascribed to Barnabas, now complete in the original; the short Epistle of Polycarp to the Philippians, and the Epistles (of very doubtful genuineness) attributed to Ignatius; an allegorical work, *the Shepherd* of Hermas, which nowhere quotes either the Old Testament or the New; a curious romance, the *Clementine Homilies;* and the writings of the Christian Apologists, Justin Martyr, Tatian, Theophilus, Athenagoras, Hermias, who, in addressing heathens, could not be expected to talk about Matthew, Mark, Luke, and John, which would be to them names without significance,— these few documents constitute nearly all the literature of the period. As we should not expect the Gospels to be quoted by name in the writings of the Apologists, though we do find John expressly mentioned by Theophilus, so in such a discussion as that of Justin Martyr with Trypho the Jew, Justin could not cite in direct proof of his doctrines works the authority of which the Jew would not recognize, though he might use them, as he does, in attestation of historic facts which he regarded as fulfilling prophecies of the Old Testament.

The author of *Supernatural Religion*, in discussing the evidence of the use of our present Gospels in the first three quarters of the second century, proceeds on two assumptions: one, that in the first half of this century vast numbers of spurious Gospels and other writings bearing the names of Apostles and their followers were in circulation in the early Church; and the other, that we have a right to expect great accuracy of quotation from the Christian Fathers, especially when they introduce the words of Christ with such a formula as "he said" or "he taught." Now this last assumption admits of being thoroughly tested, and it contradicts the most unquestionable facts. Instead of such accuracy of quotation as is assumed as the basis of his argument, it is beyond all dispute that the Fathers often quote very loosely, from memory, abridging, transposing, paraphrasing, amplifying, substituting synonymous words or equivalent expressions, combining different passages together, and occasionally mingling their own inferences with their citations. In regard to the first assumption, a careful sifting of the evidence will show, I believe, that there is really no *proof* that in the time of Justin Martyr (with the possible exception of the Gospel according to the Hebrews, which in its primitive form may have been the Hebrew original from which our present Greek Gospel ascribed to Matthew was mainly derived) there was a single work, bearing the title of a Gospel, which as a *history of Christ's ministry* came into competition with our present four Gospels, or which took the place among Christians which our Gospels certainly held in the last quarter of the second century. Much confusion has arisen from the fact that the term "Gospel" was in ancient times applied to speculative works which gave the writer's view of the Gospel, *i.e.*, of the doctrine of Christ, or among the Gnostics, which set forth their *gnosis; e.g.*, among the followers of Basilides, Hippolytus tells us, "the Gospel" is ἡ τῶν ὑπερκοσμίων γνῶσις, "the knowledge of supermundane things" (*Ref. Hær.* vii. 27). Again, the apocryphal Gospels of the Nativity and the Infancy, or such works as the so-called Gospel of Nicodemus, describing the descent of Christ into Hades, have given popular currency to the idea that there were floating about in the middle of the second century a great number of Gospels, rival histories of Christ's ministry; which these apocryphal Gospels, however, are not and do not pretend to be. Other sources of confusion, as the blunders of writers like Epiphanius, I pass over. To enter into a discussion and elucidation of this subject here is of course impossible: I will only recommend the reading of Mr. Norton's full examination of it in the third volume of his *Genuineness of the Gospels*, which needs, to be sure, a little supplementing, but the main positions of which I believe to be impregnable.

Resting on these untenable assumptions, the author of *Supernatural Religion* subjects this early fragmentary literature to a minute examination, and explains away what seem to be quotations from or references to our present Gospels in these different works as borrowed from some of the multitudinous Gospels which he assumes to have been current among the early Christians, especially if these quotations and references do not present a perfect verbal correspondence with our present Gospels, as is the case with the great majority of them. Even if the correspondence is verbally exact, this proves nothing, in his view; for the quotations of the words of Jesus might be borrowed from other current Gospels which resembled ours as much as Matthew, Mark, and Luke resemble each other. But, if the verbal agreement is *not* exact, we have in his judgment a strong proof that the quotations are derived from some apocryphal book. So he comes to the conclusion that there is no certain trace of the existence of our present Gospels for about one hundred and fifty years after the death of Christ; *i.e.*, we will say, till about A.D. 180.

But here a question naturally arises: How is it, if no trace of their existence is previously discoverable, that our four Gospels are suddenly found toward the end of the second century to be received as sacred books throughout the whole Christian world? His reply is, "It is totally unnecessary for me to account for this."* He stops his investigation of the subject just at the point where we have solid facts, not conjectures, to build upon. When he comes out of the twilight into the full blaze of day, he shuts his eyes, and refuses to see anything. Such a procedure cannot be satisfactory to a sincere inquirer after the truth. The fallacy of this mode of reasoning is so well illustrated by Mr. Norton, that I must quote a few sentences. He says:—

About the end of the second century the Gospels were reverenced as sacred books by a community dispersed over the world, composed of men of different nations and languages. There were, to say the least, sixty thousand copies of them in existence; † they were read in the

---

* *Supernatural Religion*, 6th edition (1875), and 7th edition (1879), vol. i. p. ix. (Preface.)
† See Norton's *Genuineness of the Gospels*, 2d ed., i. 45-54.

churches of Christians; they were continually quoted, and appealed to, as of the highest authority; their reputation was as well established among believers from one end of the Christian community to the other, as it is at the present day among Christians in any country. But it is asserted that before that period we find no trace of their existence; and it is, therefore, inferred that they were not in common use, and but little known, even if extant in their present form. This reasoning is of the same kind as if one were to say that the first mention of Egyptian Thebes is in the time of Homer. He, indeed, describes it as a city which poured a hundred armies from its hundred gates; but his is the first mention of it, and therefore we have no reason to suppose that, before his time, it was a place of any considerable note.*

As regards the general reception of the four Gospels in the last quarter of the second century, however, a slight qualification is to be made. Some time in the latter half of the second century, the genuineness of the Gospel of John was denied by a few eccentric individuals (we have no ground for supposing that they formed a sect), whom Epiphanius (*Hær.* li., comp. liv.) calls *Alogi* ('Αλογοι), a nickname which has the double meaning of "deniers of the doctrine of the Logos," and "men without reason." They are probably the same persons as those of whom Irenæus speaks in one passage (*Hær.* iii. 11. § 9), but to whom he gives no name. But the fact that their difficulty with the Gospel was a doctrinal one, and that they appealed to no tradition in favor of their view; that they denied the Johannean authorship of the Apocalypse likewise, and absurdly ascribed both books to Cerinthus, who, unless all our information about him is false, could not possibly have written the Fourth Gospel, shows that they were persons of no critical judgment. Zeller admits (*Theol. Jahrb.* 1845, p. 645) that their opposition does not prove that the Gospel was not generally regarded in their time as of Apostolic origin. The fact that they ascribed the Fourth Gospel to Cerinthus, a heretic of the first century, contemporary with the Apostle John, shows that they could not pretend that this Gospel was a recent work.

Further, while the Gnostics generally agreed with the

---

* *Evidences of the Genuineness of the Gospels*, second edition, vol. i. pp. 195, 196.

Catholic Christians in receiving the four Gospels, and especially the Gospel of John, which the Valentinians, as Irenæus tells us, used *plenissime* (*Hær.* iii. 11. § 7), the Marcionites are an exception. They did not, however, question the genuineness of the Gospels, but regarded their authors as under the influence of Jewish prejudices. Marcion therefore rejected all but Luke, the Pauline Gospel, and cut out from this whatever he deemed objectionable. We may note here, incidentally, that the author of *Supernatural Religion*, in the first six editions of his work, contended, in opposition to the strongest evidence, that Marcion's Gospel, instead of being, as all ancient testimony represents it, a mutilated Luke, was the earlier, original Gospel, of which Luke's was a later amplification. This theory was started by Semler, that *varium, mutabile et mirabile capitulum*, as he is called by a German writer (Matthæi, *N.T. Gr.*, i. 687); and after having been adopted by Eichhorn and many German critics was so thoroughly refuted by Hilgenfeld in 1850, and especially by Volkmar in 1852, that it was abandoned by the most eminent of its former supporters, as Ritschl, Zeller, and partially by Baur. But individuals differ widely in their power of resisting evidence opposed to their prejudices, and the author of *Supernatural Religion* has few equals in this capacity. We may therefore feel that something in these interminable discussions is settled, when we note the fact that *he* has at last surrendered. His conversion is due to Dr. Sanday, who in an article in the *Fortnightly Review* (June, 1875, p. 855, ff.), reproduced in substance in his work on *The Gospels in the Second Century*, introduced the linguistic argument, showing that the very numerous and remarkable peculiarities of language and style which characterize the parts of Luke which Marcion retained are found so fully and completely in those which he rejected as to render diversity of authorship utterly incredible.

But to return to our first point,— the unquestioned reception of our present Gospels throughout the Christian world in the last quarter of the second century, and that, I add, without the least trace of any previous controversy on the subject, with the insignificant exception of the Alogi whom I have mentioned. This fact has a most important bearing on the next question in order; namely, whether the Apostolical Memoirs to which Justin Martyr appeals about the middle of the second century were or were not our four Gospels. To discuss this question fully would require a volume. All that I propose now is to place the subject in the light of acknowledged facts, and to illustrate the falsity of the premises from which the author of *Supernatural Religion* reasons.

THE writings of Justin consist of two Apologies or Defences of Christians and Christianity addressed to the Roman Emperor and Senate, the first written most probably about the year 146 or 147 (though many place it in the year 138), and a Dialogue in defence of Christianity with Trypho the Jew, written somewhat later (*Dial.* c. 120, comp. *Apol.* i. c. 26).*

In these writings, addressed, it is to be observed, to unbelievers, he quotes, not in proof of doctrines, but as authority for his account of the teaching of Christ and the facts in his life, certain works of which he commonly speaks as the "Memoirs" or "Memorabilia" of Christ, using the Greek word, Ἀπομνημονεύματα, with which we are familiar as the designation of the Memorabilia of Socrates by Xenophon. Of these books he commonly speaks as the "Memoirs by the Apostles," using this expression eight times; † four times he calls them "the Memoirs" simply; ‡ once, "Memoirs made by the Apostles which are called Gospels" (*Apol.* i. 66); once, when he cites a passage apparently from the Gospel of Luke, " Memoirs composed by the Apostles of Christ and their companions," — literally, "those who followed with them" (*Dial.* c. 103); once again (*Dial.* c. 106), when he speaks of our Saviour as changing the name of Peter, and of his giving to James and John the name Boanerges, a fact only mentioned

---

* See Engelhardt, *Das Christenthum Justins des Märtyrers* (1878), p. 71 ff.; Renan, *L'Eglise chrétienne* (1879), p. 367, n. 4.

† *Apol.* i. 67; *Dial.* cc. 100, 101, 102, 103, 104, 106 *bis*: τὰ ἀπομνημονεύματα τῶν ἀποστόλων (τῶν ἀποστ. αὐτοῦ, sc. Χριστοῦ, 5 times).

‡ *Dial.* cc. 105 *ter*, 107.

so far as we know in the Gospel of Mark, he designates as his authority "Peter's Memoirs," which, supposing him to have used our Gospels, is readily explained by the fact that Peter was regarded by the ancients as furnishing the materials for the Gospel of Mark, his travelling companion and interpreter.* Once more, Justin speaks in the plural of "those who have written Memoirs," οἱ ἀπομνημονεύσαντες, "of all things concerning our Saviour Jesus Christ, whom we believe" (*Apol.* i. 33); and, again, "the Apostles wrote" so and so, referring to an incident mentioned in all four of the Gospels (*Dial.* c. 88).

But the most important fact mentioned in Justin's writings respecting these Memoirs, which he describes as " composed by Apostles of Christ and their companions," appears in his account of Christian worship, in the sixty-seventh chapter of his First Apology. "On the day called Sunday," he says, "all who live in cities or in the country gather together to one place, and the Memoirs by the Apostles or the writings of the Prophets are read, as long as time permits. When the reader has finished, the president admonishes and exhorts to the imitation of these good things." It appears, then, that, at the time when he wrote, these books, whatever they were, on which he relied for his knowledge of Christ's teaching and life, were held in at least as high reverence as the writings of the Prophets, were read in the churches just as our Gospels were in the last quarter of the second century, and formed the basis of the hortatory discourse that followed. The writings of the Prophets might alternate with them in this use; but Justin mentions the Memoirs first.

These "Memoirs," then, were well-known books, distin-

---

* I adopt with most scholars (*versus* Semisch and Grimm) the construction which refers the αὐτοῦ in this passage not to Christ, but to Peter, in accordance with the use of the genitive after ἀπομνημονεύματα everywhere else in Justin. (See a note on the question in the *Christian Examiner* for July, 1854, lvi. 128 f.) For the statement in the text, see Tertullian, *Adv. Marc.* iv. 5.: Licet et Marcus quod edidit [evangelium] Petri affirmetur, cujus interpres Marcus. Jerome, *De Vir. ill.* c. 1.: Sed et Evangelium juxta Marcum, qui auditor ejus [sc. Petri] et interpres fuit, hujus dicitur. Comp. *ibid.* c. 8, and *Ep.* 120 (al. 150) *ad Hedib.* c. 11. See also Papias, ap. Euseb. *Hist. Eccl.* iii. 39; Irenæus, *Hær.* iii. 1, § 1 (ap. Euseb. v. 8); 10, § 6; Clement of Alexandria ap. Euseb. ii. 15; vi. 14; Origen ap. Euseb. vi. 25; and the striking passage of Eusebius, *Dem. Evang.* iii. 3, pp. 120^d–122^a, quoted by Lardner, *Works* iv. 91 ff. (Lond. 1829).

guished from others as the authoritative source of instruction concerning the doctrine and life of Christ.

There is one other coincidence between the language which Justin uses in describing these books and that which we find in the generation following. The four Gospels as a collection might indifferently be called, and were indifferently cited as, "the Gospels" or "the Gospel." We find this use of the expression "the Gospel" in Theophilus of Antioch, Irenæus, Clement of Alexandria, Origen, Hippolytus, the Apostolical Constitutions, Tertullian, and later writers generally.* Now Justin represents Trypho as saying, "I know that your precepts in what is called the Gospel (ἐν τῷ λεγομένῳ εὐαγγελίῳ) are so wonderful and great as to cause a suspicion that no one may be able to observe them." (*Dial.* c. 10.) In another place, he quotes, apparently, Matt. xi. 27 (comp. Luke x. 22) as being "written in the Gospel."† No plausible explanation can be given of this language except that which recognizes in it the same usage that we constantly find in later Christian writers. The books which in one place Justin calls "Gospels," books composed by Apostles and their companions, were in reference to what gave them their distinctive value *one*. They were the record of the Gospel of Christ in different forms. No *one* of our present Gospels, if these were in circulation in the time of Justin, and certainly no *one* of that great number of Gospels which

---

* See Justin or Pseudo-Justin, *De Res.* c. 10.— Ignat. or Pseudo-Ignat. *Ad Philad.* cc. 5, 8; *Smyrn.* cc. 5(?), 7.— Pseudo-Clem. 2 *Ep. ad Cor.* c. 8.— Theophil. iii. 14.— Iren. *Hær.* i. 7. §4; 8. §4; 20. §2; 27. §2. ii. 22. §5; 26. §2. iii. 5. §1; 9. §2; 10. §§2, 6; 11. §§8 (τετράμορφον τὸ εὐαγγέλιον), 9; 16. §5. iv. 20. §§6, 9; 32. §1; 34. §1.—Clem. Al. *Pæd.* i. c. 5, pp. 104, 105, *bis* ed. Potter; c. 9, pp. 143; 145 *bis*, 148. ii. 1, p. 169; c. 10, p. 235; c. 12, p. 246. *Strom.* ii. 16, p. 467. iii. 6, p. 537; c. 11, p. 544. iv. 1, p. 564; c. 4, p. 570. v. 5, p. 664. vi. 6, p. 764; c. 11, p. 784 *bis*; c. 14, p. 797. vii. 3, p. 836. *Ecl. proph.* cc. 50, 57.— Origen, *Cont. Cels.* i. 51. ii. 13, 24, 27, 34, 36, 37, 61, 63 (Opp. I. 367, 398, 409, 411, 415, 416 *bis*, 433, 434 ed. Delarue). *In Joan.* tom. i. §§4, 5. v. §4. (Opp. IV. 4, 98.) Pseudo-Orig. *Dial. de recta in Deum fide*, sect. 1 (Opp. I. 807).— Hippol. *Noët.* c. 6.—Const. Ap. i. 1, 2 *bis*, 5, 6. ii. 1 *bis*, 5 *bis*, 6 *bis*, 8, 13, 16, 17, 35, 39. iii. 7. v. 14. vi. 23 *bis*, 28. vii. 24.—Tertull. *Cast.* c. 4. *Pudic.* c. 2. *Adv. Marc.* iv. 7. *Hermog.* c. 20. *Resurr.* c. 27. *Prax.* cc. 20, 21.— PLURAL, Muratorian Canon (also the sing.).— Theophilus, *Ad Autol.* iii. 12, τὰ τῶν προφητῶν καὶ τῶν εὐαγγελίων. — Clem. Al. Strom. iv. 6. p. 582. Hippol. *Ref. Hær.* vii. 38, p. 259, τῶν δὲ εὐαγγελίων ἢ τοῦ ἀποστόλου, and later writers everywhere.— *Plural* used where the passage quoted is found in only *one* of the Gospels, Basilides ap. Hippol. *Ref. Hær.* vii. 22, 27.—Const. Ap. ii. 53.— Cyril of Jerusalem, *Procat.* c. 3; *Cat.* ii. 4; x. 1; xvi. 16.—Theodoret, *Quæst. in Num.* c. xix. q. 35, Migne lxxx. 385; *In Ps.* xlv. 16, M. lxxx. 1197; *In* 1 *Thess.* v. 15, M. lxxxii. 649, and so often.

† On this important passage see Note A at the end of this essay.

the writer of *Supernatural Religion* imagines to have been current at that period, could have been so distinguished from the rest as to be called " *the* Gospel."

It has been maintained by the author of *Supernatural Religion* and others that Justin's description of the Gospels as "Memoirs composed by *the* Apostles and those who followed with them" (to render the Greek verbally) cannot apply to works composed by *two* Apostles and two companions of Apostles: "*the* Apostles" must mean *all* the Apostles, "the collective body of the Apostles." (*S. R.* i. 291.) Well, if it must, then the connected expression, "those that followed with them" (τῶν ἐκείνοις παρακολουθησάντων), where the definite article is used in just the same way in Greek, must mean "all those that followed with them." We have, then, a truly marvellous book, if we take the view of *Supernatural Religion* that the "Memoirs" of Justin was a single work; a Gospel, namely, composed by "the collective body of the Apostles" and the collective body of those who accompanied them. If the "Memoirs" consist of several different books *thus* composed, the marvel is not lessened. Now Justin is not responsible for this absurdity. The simple fact is that the definite article in Greek in this case distinguishes the two *classes* to which the writers of the Gospels belonged.*

To state in full detail and with precision all the features of the problem presented by Justin's quotations, and his references to facts in the life of Christ, is here, of course, impossible. But what is the obvious aspect of the case?

It will not be disputed that there is a very close correspondence between the history of Christ sketched by Justin, embracing numerous details, and that found in our Gospels: the few statements not authorized by them, such as that Christ was born in a cave, that the Magi came from Arabia, that Christ as a carpenter made ploughs and yokes,

---

* For illustrations of this use of the article, see Norton's *Evidences of the Genuineness of the Gospels*, 1st ed. (1837), vol. i. p. 190, note. Comp. 1 Thess. ii. 14 and Jude 17, where it would be idle to suppose that the writer means that *all* the Apostles had given the particular warning referred to. See also Origen, *Cont. Cels.* i. 51, p. 367, μετὰ τὴν ἀναγεγραμμένην ἐν τοῖς εὐαγγελίοις ὑπὸ τῶν Ἰησοῦ μαθητῶν ἱστορίαν; and ii. 13, παραπλήσια τοῖς ὑπὸ τῶν μαθητῶν τοῦ Ἰησοῦ γραφεῖσιν. See, further, Note B at the end of this essay.

present little or no objection to the supposition that they were his main authority. These details may be easily explained as founded on oral tradition, or as examples of that substitution of *inferences* from facts for the facts themselves, which we find in so many ancient and modern writers, and observe in every-day life.* Again, there is a substantial correspondence between the teaching of Christ as reported by Justin and that found in the Gospels. Only one or two sayings are ascribed to Christ by Justin which are not contained in the Gospels, and these may naturally be referred, like others which we find in writers who received our four Gospels as alone authoritative, to oral tradition, or may have been taken from some writing or writings now lost which contained such traditions.† That Justin actually used all our present Gospels is admitted by Hilgenfeld and Keim. But that they were not his main authority is argued chiefly from the want of exact verbal correspondence between his citations of the words of Christ and the language of our Gospels, where the meaning is essentially the same. The untenableness of this argument has been demonstrated, I conceive, by Norton, Semisch, Westcott, and Sanday, *versus* Hilgenfeld and *Supernatural Religion*. Its weakness is illustrated in a Note at the end of this essay, and will be further illustrated presently by the full discussion of a passage of special interest and importance. Justin nowhere expressly

---

* Several of Justin's additions in the way of detail seem to have proceeded from his *assumption* of the fulfilment of Old Testament prophecies, or what he regarded as such. See Semisch, *Die apost. Denkwürdigkeiten des Märtyrers Justinus* (1848), p. 377 ff.; Volkmar, *Der Ursprung unserer Evangelien* (1866), p. 124 f.; Westcott, *Canon of the N. T.*, p. 162, 4th ed. (1875), and Dr. E. A. Abbott, art. *Gospels* in the ninth ed. of the Encyclopædia Britannica (p. 817), who remarks: "Justin never quotes any rival Gospel, nor alleges any words or facts which make it probable he used a rival Gospel; such non-canonical sayings and facts as he mentions are readily explicable as the results of lapse of memory, general looseness and inaccuracy, extending to the use of the Old as well as the New Testament, and the desire to adapt the facts of the New Scriptures to the prophecies of the Old." (p. 818).

† See Westcott, "On the Apocryphal Traditions of the Lord's Words and Works," appended to his *Introd. to the Study of the Gospels*, 5th ed. (1875), pp. 453-461, and the little volume of J. T. Dodd, *Sayings ascribed to our Lord by the Fathers*, etc., Oxford, 1874. Compare Norton, *Genuineness of the Gospels*, 2d ed., i. 220 ff. The stress which the author of *Supernatural Religion* lays on the word πάντα in the passage (*Apol.* i. 33) where Justin speaks of "those who have written memoirs of *all things* concerning our Saviour Jesus Christ" shows an extraordinary disregard of the common use of such expressions. It is enough to compare, as Westcott does, Acts i. 1. For illustrations from Justin (*Apol.* ii. 6; i. 45; *Dial.* cc. 44, 121) sée Semisch, *Die apost. Denkwürdigkeiten* u. s. w., p. 404 f.

quotes the "Memoirs" for anything which is not substantially found in our Gospels; and there is nothing in his deviations from exact correspondence with them, as regards matters of fact, or the report of the words of Christ, which may not be abundantly paralleled in the writings of the Christian Fathers who used our four Gospels as alone authoritative.

With this view of the state of the case, and of the character of the books used and described by Justin though without naming their authors, let us now consider the bearing of the indisputable fact (with which the author of *Supernatural Religion* thinks he has no concern) of the general reception of our four Gospels as genuine in the last quarter of the second century. As I cannot state the argument more clearly or more forcibly than it has been done by Mr. Norton, I borrow his language. Mr. Norton says:—

> The manner in which Justin speaks of the character and authority of the books to which he appeals, of their reception among Christians, and of the use which was made of them, proves these books to have been the Gospels. They carried with them the authority of the Apostles. They were those writings from which he and other Christians derived their knowledge of the history and doctrines of Christ. They were relied upon by him as primary and decisive evidence in his explanations of the character of Christianity. They were regarded as sacred books. They were read in the assemblies of Christians on the Lord's day, in connection with the Prophets of the Old Testament. Let us now consider the manner in which the Gospels were regarded by the contemporaries of Justin. Irenæus was in the vigor of life before Justin's death; and the same was true of very many thousands of Christians living when Irenæus wrote. But he tells us that the four Gospels are the four pillars of the Church, the foundation of Christian faith, written by those who had first orally preached the Gospel, by two Apostles and two companions of Apostles. It is incredible that Irenæus and Justin should have spoken of different books. We cannot suppose that writings, such as the Memoirs of which Justin speaks, believed to be the works of Apostles and companions of Apostles, read in Christian Churches, and received as sacred books, of the highest authority, should, immediately after he wrote, have fallen into neglect and oblivion, and been superseded by another set of books. The strong sentiment of their value could not so silently, and so unaccountably, have changed into entire disregard, and have been transferred to other writings. The copies of them spread over the world could not so suddenly and mysteriously have disappeared,

that no subsequent trace of their existence should be clearly discoverable. When, therefore, we find Irenæus, the contemporary of Justin, ascribing to the four Gospels the same character, the same authority, and the same authors, as are ascribed by Justin to the Memoirs quoted by him, which were called Gospels, there can be no reasonable doubt that the Memoirs of Justin were the Gospels of Irenæus.*

It may be objected to Mr. Norton's argument, that "many writings which have been excluded from the canon were publicly read in the churches, until very long after Justin's day." (*S.R.* i. 294.) The author of *Supernatural Religion* mentions particularly the Epistle of the Roman Clement to the Corinthians, the Epistle of Soter, the Bishop of Rome, to the Corinthians, the "Pastor" or "Shepherd" of Hermas, and the Apocalypse of Peter. To these may be added the Epistle ascribed to Barnabas.

To give the objection any force, the argument must run thus: The writings above named were at one time generally regarded by Christians as sacred books, of the highest authority and importance, and placed at least on a level with the writings of the prophets of the Old Testament. They were afterwards excluded from the canon: therefore a similar change might take place among Christians in their estimate of the writings which Justin has described under the name of "Memoirs by the Apostles." In the course of thirty years, a different set of books might silently supersede them in the whole Christian world.

The premises are false. There is no proof that any one of these writings was ever regarded as possessing the same authority and value as Justin's "Memoirs," or anything like it. From the very nature of the case, books received as authentic records of the life and teaching of CHRIST must have had an importance which could belong to no others. On the character of the teaching and the facts of the life of Christ as recorded in the "Memoirs," Justin's whole argument rests. Whether he regarded the Apostolic writings as "inspired" or not, he unquestionably regarded CHRIST as inspired, or rather as the divine, inspiring Logos (*Apol.* i.

---

* *Evidences of the Genuineness of the Gospels*, 2d ed., vol. i. pp. 237–239.

33, 36; ii. 10); and his teaching as "the new law," universal, everlasting, which superseded "the old covenant." (See *Dial.* cc. 11, 12, etc.) The books that contained this were to the Christians of Justin's time the very foundation of their faith.

As to the works mentioned by *Supernatural Religion,* not only is there no evidence that any one of them ever held a place in the Christian Church to be compared for a moment with that of the Gospels, but there is abundant evidence to the contrary. They were read in some churches for a time as edifying books,— the Epistle of Clement of Rome "in very many churches" according to Eusebius (*Hist. Eccl.* iii. 16),— and a part of them were regarded by a few Christian writers as having apostolic or semi-apostolic authority, or as divinely inspired. One of the most definite statements about them is that of Dionysius of Corinth (*cir.* A.D. 175–180), who, in a letter to the church at Rome (Euseb. *Hist. Eccl.* iv. 23), tells us that the Epistle of Soter (d. 176?) to the Christians at Corinth was read in their church for edification or "admonition" ($νουθετεῖσθαι$ is the word used) on a certain Sunday, and would continue to be so read from time to time, as the Epistle of Clement had been. This shows how far the occasional public reading of such a writing in the church was from implying its canonical authority.— Clement of Alexandria repeatedly quotes the Epistle ascribed to Barnabas as the work of "Barnabas the Apostle," but criticises and condemns one of his interpretations (*Strom.* ii. 15, p. 464), and in another place, as Mr. Norton remarks, rejects a fiction found in the work (*Pæd.* ii. 10, p. 220, ff.).— "The Shepherd" of Hermas in its *form* claims to be a divine vision; its allegorical character suited the taste of many; and the Muratorian Canon (*cir.* A.D. 170) says that it ought to be read in the churches, but not as belonging to the writings of the prophets or apostles. (See Credner, *Gesch. d. neutest. Kanon,* p. 165.) This was the general view of those who did not reject it as altogether apocryphal. It appears in the Sinaitic MS. as an appendix to the New Testament.—The Apocalypse of Peter appears to have imposed upon some as the work of the Apostle. The Muratorian Canon says, "Some among us are unwilling that it should be read in the church." It seems to have been received as genuine by Clement of Alexandria (*Ecl. proph.* cc. 41, 48, 49) and Methodius (*Conv.* ii. 6). Besides these, the principal writers who speak of it are Eusebius (*Hist. Eccl.* iii. 3. § 2; 25. § 4; vi. 14. § 1), who rejects it as uncanonical or spurious, Jerome (*De Vir. ill.* c. 1), who puts it among apocryphal writings, and Sozomen (*Hist. Eccl.* vii. 19), who mentions that, though rejected by the ancients as spurious, it was read once a year in some churches of Palestine.*

It appears sufficiently from what has been said that there is nothing in the limited ecclesiastical use of these books, or in the over-estimate of their authority and value by some individuals, to detract from the force of Mr. Norton's argument. *Supernatural Religion* here confounds things that differ very widely.†

At this stage of the argument, we are entitled, I think, to come to the examination of the apparent use of the Gospel of John by Justin Martyr with a strong presumption in favor of the view that this apparent use is real. In other words, there is a very strong presumption that the "Memoirs" used by Justin and called by him "Gospels" and collectively "the Gospel," and described as "composed by Apostles of Christ and their companions," were actually our present Gospels, composed by two Apostles and two companions of Apostles. This presumption is, I believe, greatly strengthened by the evidence of the use of the Fourth Gospel by writers between the time of Justin Martyr and Irenæus, and also by the evidences of its use before the time of Justin by the Gnostic sects. But, leaving those topics for the present, we will consider the direct evidence of its use by Justin.

The first passage noticed will be examined pretty thoroughly: both because the discussion of it will serve to illustrate the false reasoning of the author of *Supernatural Relig-*

---

* See, on this book, Hilgenfeld, *Nov. Test. extra canonem receptum* (1866), iv. 74, ff.

† On this whole subject, see Semisch, *Die apostol. Denkwürdigkeiten des Märt. Justinus,* p. 61, ff.

ion and other writers respecting the quotations of Justin Martyr which agree in substance with passages in our Gospels while differing in the form of expression; and because it is of special importance in its bearing on the question whether Justin made use of the Fourth Gospel, and seems to me, when carefully examined, to be in itself almost decisive.

The passage is that in which Justin gives an account of Christian baptism, in the sixty-first chapter of his First Apology. Those who are ready to make a Christian profession, he says, "are brought by us to a place where there is water, and in the manner of being born again [*or* regenerated] in which we ourselves also were born again, they are born again; for in the name of the Father of the universe and sovereign God, and of our Saviour Jesus Christ, and of the Holy Spirit, they then receive the bath in the water. For Christ also said, Except ye be born again, ye shall in no wise enter into the kingdom of heaven (Ἂν μὴ ἀναγεννηθῆτε, οὐ μὴ εἰσέλθητε εἰς τὴν βασιλείαν τῶν οὐρανῶν). But that it is impossible for those who have once been born to enter into the wombs of those who brought them forth is manifest to all."

The passage in the Gospel of John of which this reminds us is found in chap. iii. 3–5: "Jesus answered and said to him [Nicodemus], Verily, verily I say unto thee, Except a man be born anew, he cannot see the kingdom of God ('Ἐὰν μή τις γεννηθῇ ἄνωθεν, οὐ δύναται ἰδεῖν τὴν βασιλείαν τοῦ θεοῦ). Nicodemus saith to him, How can a man be born when he is old? Can he enter a second time into his mother's womb and be born? Jesus answered, Verily, verily I say unto thee, Except a man be born of water and the Spirit, he cannot enter into the kingdom of God" ('Ἐὰν μή τις γεννηθῇ ἐξ ὕδατος καὶ πνεύματος, οὐ δύναται εἰσελθεῖν εἰς τὴν βασιλείαν τοῦ θεοῦ). Compare verse 7, "Marvel not that I said unto thee, Ye must be born anew" (δεῖ ὑμᾶς γεννηθῆναι ἄνωθεν); and Matt. xviii. 3, "Verily I say unto you, Except ye be changed, and become as little children, ye shall in no wise enter into the kingdom of heaven" (οὐ μὴ εἰσέλθητε εἰς τὴν βασιλείαν τῶν οὐρανῶν).

I have rendered the Greek as literally as possible; but it

should be observed that the word translated "anew," ἄνωθεν, might also be rendered "from above." This point will be considered hereafter.

Notwithstanding the want of verbal correspondence, I believe that we have here in Justin a free quotation from the Gospel of John, modified a little by a reminiscence of Matt. xviii. 3.

The first thing that strikes us in Justin's quotation is the fact that the remark with which it concludes, introduced by Justin as if it were a grave observation of his own, is simply silly in the connection in which it stands. In John, on the other hand, where it is not to be understood as a serious question, it admits, as we shall see, of a natural explanation as the language of Nicodemus. This shows, as everything else shows, the weakness (to use no stronger term) of Volkmar's hypothesis, that John has here borrowed from Justin, not Justin from John. The observation affords also, by its very remarkable peculiarity, strong evidence that Justin derived it, together with the declaration which accompanies it, from the Fourth Gospel.

It will be well, before proceeding to our immediate task, to consider the meaning of the passage in John, and what the real difficulty of Nicodemus was. He could not have been perplexed by the figurative use of the expression "to be born anew": that phraseology was familiar to the Jews to denote the change which took place in a Gentile when he became a proselyte to Judaism.* But the unqualified language of our Saviour, expressing a universal necessity, implied that even the Jewish Pharisee, with all his pride of sanctity and superior knowledge, must experience a radical change, like that which a Gentile proselyte to Judaism underwent, before he could enjoy the blessings of the Messiah's kingdom. This was what amazed Nicodemus. Pretending therefore to take the words in their literal meaning, he asks, "How can a man be born when he is old? Can he enter," etc. He imposes an absurd and ridiculous sense on the

---

* See Lightfoot and Wetstein, or T. Robinson or Wünsche, on John iii. 3 or 5.

words, to lead Jesus to explain himself further.* Thus viewed, the question is to some purpose in John; while the language in Justin, as a serious proposition, is idle, and betrays its non-originality.

The great difference in the form of expression between Justin's citation and the Gospel of John is urged as decisive against the supposition that he has here used this Gospel. It is observed further that all the deviations of Justin from the language of the Fourth Gospel are also found in a quotation of the words of Christ in the Clementine Homilies; and hence it has been argued that Justin and the writer of the Clementines quoted from the same apocryphal Gospel, perhaps the Gospel according to the Hebrews or the Gospel according to Peter. In the Clementine Homilies (xi. 26), the quotation runs as follows: "For thus the prophet swore unto us, saying, Verily I say unto you, except ye be born again by living water into the name of Father, Son, Holy Spirit, ye shall in no wise enter into the kingdom of heaven." But it will be seen at once that the author of the Clementines differs as widely from Justin as Justin from the Fourth Gospel, and that there is no plausibility in the supposition that he and Justin quoted from the same apocryphal book. The quotation in the Clementines is probably only a free combination of the language in John iii. 3–5 with Matt. xxviii. 19, modified somewhat in form by the influence of Matt. xviii. 3.† Such combinations of different passages, and such quotations of the words of Christ according to the sense rather than the letter, are not uncommon in the Fathers. Or, the Clementines may have used Justin.

I now propose to show in detail that the differences in form between Justin's quotation and the phraseology of the Fourth Gospel, marked as they are, all admit of an easy and natural explanation on the supposition that he really borrowed from it, and that they are paralleled by similar variations in the

---

* See Norton, *A New Trans. of the Gospels, with Notes*, vol. ii. p. 507.

† On the quotations from the Gospel of John as well as from the other Gospels in the Clementine Homilies, see Sanday, *The Gospels in the Second Century*, pp. 288–295; comp. pp. 161–187. See also Westcott, *Canon of the N. T.*, pp. 282–288; and comp. pp. 150–156.

quotations of the same passage by Christian writers who used our four Gospels as their exclusive authority. If this is made clear, the fallacy of the assumption on which the author of *Supernatural Religion* reasons in his remarks on this passage, and throughout his discussion of Justin's quotations, will be apparent. He has argued on an assumption of verbal accuracy in the quotations of the Christian Fathers which is baseless, and which there were peculiar reasons for not expecting from Justin in such works as his Apologies.*

Let us take up the differences point by point: —

1. The solemn introduction, "Verily, verily I say unto thee," is omitted. But this would be very naturally omitted: (1) because it is of no importance for the sense; and (2) because the Hebrew words used, Ἀμὴν ἀμήν, would be unintelligible to the Roman Emperor, without a particular explanation (compare *Apol.* i. 65). (3) It is usually omitted by Christian writers in quoting the passage: so, for example, by the DOCETIST in HIPPOLYTUS (*Ref. Hær.* viii. 10, p. 267), IRENÆUS (Frag. 35, ed. Stieren, 33 Harvey), ORIGEN, in a Latin version (*In Ex. Hom.* v. 1, Opp. ii. 144, ed. Delarue; *In Ep. ad Rom.* lib. v. c. 8, Opp. iv. 560), the APOSTOLICAL CONSTITUTIONS (vi. 15), EUSEBIUS twice (*In Isa.* i. 16, 17, and iii. 1, 2; Migne xxiv. 96, 109), ATHANASIUS (*De Incarn.* c. 14, Opp. i. 59, ed. Montf.), CYRIL OF JERUSALEM twice (*Cat.* iii. 4; xvii. 11), BASIL THE GREAT (*Adv. Eunom.* lib. v. Opp. i. 308 (437), ed. Benedict.), PSEUDO-BASIL three times (*De Bapt.* i. 2. §§ 2, 6; ii. 1. § 1; Opp. ii. 630 (896), 633 (899), 653 (925)), GREGORY NYSSEN (*De Christi Bapt.* Opp. iii. 369), EPHRAEM SYRUS (*De Pœnit.* Opp. iii. 183), MACARIUS ÆGYP-

---

*On the whole subject of Justin Martyr's quotations, I would refer to the admirably clear, forcible, and accurate statement of the case in Norton's *Evidences of the Genuineness of the Gospels*, 2d ed., vol. i. pp. 200-239, and Addit. Note E, pp. ccxiv.-ccxxxviii. His account is less detailed than that of Semisch, Hilgenfeld, and *Supernatural Religion*, but is thoroughly trustworthy. On one point there may be a doubt: Mr. Norton says that "Justin twice gives the words, *Thou art my son; this day have I begotten thee*, as those uttered at our Saviour's baptism; and in one place says expressly that the words were found in the Memoirs by the Apostles." This last statement seems to me incorrect. The quotations referred to will be found in *Dial. c. Tryph.* cc. 88, 103; but in neither case does Justin *say*, according to the grammatical construction of his language, that the words in question were found in the Memoirs, though it is probable that they were. The discussion of Justin's quotations by Professor Westcott and Dr. Sanday in the works referred to in the preceding note is also valuable, especially in reference to the early variations in the text of the Gospels.

TIUS (*Hom.* xxx. 3), CHRYSOSTOM (*De consubst.* vii. 3, Opp. i. 505 (618), ed. Montf.; *In Gen. Serm.* vii. 5, Opp. iv. 681 (789), and elsewhere repeatedly), THEODORET (*Quæst. in Num.* 35, Migne lxxx. 385), BASIL OF SELEUCIA (*Orat.* xxviii. 3, Migne lxxxv. 321), and a host of other writers, both Greek and Latin,— I could name *forty*, if necessary.

2. The change of the indefinite τις, in the singular, to the second person plural: "Except *a man* be born anew" to "Except *ye* be born anew." This also is unimportant. This is shown, and the origin of the change is partially explained (1) by the fact, not usually noticed, that it is made *by the speaker himself in the Gospel*, in professedly repeating in the seventh verse the words used in the third; the indefinite singular involving, and being equivalent to, the plural. Verse 7 reads: "Marvel not that I *said* unto thee, *Ye* must be born anew." (2) The second person plural would also be suggested by the similar passage in Matt. xviii. 3, "Except *ye* be changed and become as little children, *ye* shall in no wise enter into the kingdom of heaven." Nothing was more natural than that in a quotation from memory the language of these two kindred passages should be somewhat mixed; and such a confusion of similar passages is frequent in the writings of the Fathers. This affords an easy explanation also of Justin's substituting, in agreement with Matthew, "shall in no wise enter" for "cannot enter," and "kingdom of heaven" for "kingdom of God." The two passages of John and Matthew are actually mixed together in a somewhat similar way in a free quotation by CLEMENT OF ALEXANDRIA, a writer who unquestionably used our Gospels alone as authoritative,—"the four Gospels, which," as he says, "*have been handed down* to us" (*Strom.* iii. 13, p. 553).*
(3) This declaration of Christ would often be quoted in the early Christian preaching, in reference to the importance of baptism; and the second person plural would thus be natu-

---

* Clement (*Cohort. ad Gentes*, c. 9, p. 69) blends Matt. xviii. 3 and John iii. 3 as follows: "Except ye again become as little children, and *be born again* (ἀναγεννηθῆτε), as the Scripture saith, ye will in no wise receive him who is truly your Father, and will in no wise ever enter into the kingdom of heaven."

rally substituted for the indefinite singular, to give greater directness to the exhortation. So in the CLEMENTINE HOMILIES (xi. 26), and in both forms of the CLEMENTINE EPITOME (c. 18, pp. 16, 134, ed. Dressel, Lips. 1859). (4) That this change of number and person does not imply the use of an apocryphal Gospel is further shown by the fact that it is made twice in quoting the passage by Jeremy Taylor, who in a third quotation also substitutes the plural for the singular in a somewhat different way.* (See below, p. 40.)

3. The change of ἐὰν μή τις γεννηθῇ ἄνωθεν, verse 3 (or γεννηθῇ merely, verse 5), "Except a man be born anew," or "over again," into ἂν μὴ ἀναγεννηθῆτε, "Except ye be born again," or "regenerated"; in other words, the substitution of ἀναγεννᾶσθαι for γεννᾶσθαι ἄνωθεν, or for the simple verb in verse 5, presents no real difficulty, though much has been made of it. (1) It is said that γεννᾶσθαι ἄνωθεν cannot mean "to be born *anew*," but must mean "to be born *from above*." But we have the clearest philological evidence that ἄνωθεν has the meaning of "anew," "over again," as well as "from above." In the only passage in a classical author where the precise phrase, γεννᾶσθαι ἄνωθεν, has been pointed out, namely, Artemidorus on Dreams, i. 13, ed. Reiff (al. 14), it cannot possibly have any other meaning. Meyer, who rejects this sense, has fallen into a strange mistake about the passage in Artemidorus, showing that he cannot have looked at it. Meaning "from above" or "from the top" (Matt. xxvii. 51), then "from the beginning" (Luke i. 3), ἄνωθεν is used, with πάλιν to strengthen

---

* Professor James Drummond well remarks: "How easily such a change might be made, when verbal accuracy was not studied, is instructively shewn in Theophylact's paraphrase [I translate the Greek]: 'But I say unto thee, that both thou and every other man whatsoever, unless having been born from above [*or* anew] and of God, *ye* receive the true faith [*lit.* the worthy opinion] concerning me, are outside of the kingdom.'" Chrysostom (also cited by Prof. Drummond) observes that Christ's words are equivalent to ἐὰν σὺ μὴ γεννηθῇ κ.τ.λ., "Except *thou* be born," etc., but are put in the indefinite form in order to make the discourse less offensive. I gladly take this opportunity to call attention to the valuable article by Prof. Drummond in the *Theological Review* for October, 1875, vol. xii. pp. 471-488, "On the alleged Quotation from the Fourth Gospel relating to the New Birth, in Justin Martyr, *Apol.* i. c. 61." He has treated the question with the ability, candor, and cautious accuracy of statement which distinguish his writings generally. For the quotation given above, see p. 476 of the *Review*. I am indebted to him for several valuable suggestions; but, to prevent misapprehension as to the extent of this indebtedness, I may be permitted to refer to my note on the subject in the American edition of Smith's *Dictionary of the Bible*, vol. ii. p. 1433, published in 1869, six years before the appearance of Prof. Drummond's article.

it, to signify "again from the beginning," "all over again" (Gal. iv. 9, where see the passages from Galen and Hippocrates cited by Wetstein, and Wisd. of Sol. xix. 6, where see Grimm's note), like πάλιν ἐκ δευτέρου or δεύτερον (Matt. xxvi. 42, John xxi. 16), and in the classics πάλιν αὖ, πάλιν αὖθις, πάλιν ἐξ ἀρχῆς. Thus it gets the meaning "anew," "over again"; see the passages cited by McClellan in his note on John iii. 3.* (2) Ἄνωθεν was here understood as meaning "again" by the translators of many of the ancient versions; namely, the Old Latin, "denuo," the Vulgate, Coptic, Peshito Syriac (*Sup. Rel.*, 6th edit., is mistaken about this), Æthiopic, Georgian (see Malan's *The Gospel according to St. John*, etc.). (3) The Christian Fathers who prefer the other interpretation, as Origen, Cyril of Alexandria, and Theophylact, recognize the fact that the word may have either meaning. The ambiguity is also noticed by Chrysostom. (4) Ἀναγεννᾶσθαι was the common word in Christian literature to describe the change referred to. So already in 1 Pet. i. 3, 23; comp. 1 Pet. ii. 2; and see the context in Justin. (5) This meaning best suits the connection. Verse 4 represents it as so understood by Nicodemus: "Can he enter *a second time*," etc. The fact that John has used the word ἄνωθεν in two other passages in a totally different connection (viz. iii. 31, xix. 11) in the sense of "from above" is of little weight. He has nowhere else used it in reference to the new birth to denote that it is a birth from above: to express that idea, he has used a differ-

---

*The passages are: Joseph. *Ant.* i. 18, § 3; Socrates in Stobæus, *Flor.* cxxiv. 41, iv. 135 Meineke; Harpocration, *Lex.* s. v. ἀναδικάσασθαι; Pseudo-Basil, *De Bapt.* i. 2. § 7; Can. Apost. 46, al. 47, al. 39; to which add Origen, *In Joan.* tom. xx. c. 12, Opp. iv. 322, who gives the words of Christ to Peter in the legend found in the Acts of Paul: ἄνωθεν μέλλω σταυρωθῆναι = "*iterum* crucifigi." I have verified McClellan's references (*The N.T.* etc. vol. 1. p. 284, Lond. 1875), and given them in a form in which they may be more easily found.

Though many of the best commentators take ἄνωθεν here in the sense of "from above," as Bengel, Lücke, De Wette, Meyer, Clausen, and so the lexicographers Wahl, Bretschneider, Robinson, the rendering "anew" is supported by Chrysostom, Nonnus, Euthymius, Luther, Calvin, Beza, Grotius, Wetstein, Kypke, Krebs, Knapp (*Scripta var. Arg.* i. 188, ed. 2da), Kuinoel, Credner (*Beiträge*, i. 253), Olshausen, Tholuck, Neander, Norton, Noyes, Alford, Ewald, Hofmann, Luthardt, Weiss, Godet, Farrar, Watkins, Westcott, and the recent lexicographers, Grimm and Cremer. The word is not to be understood as merely equivalent to "again," "a second time," but implies an entire change. Compare the use of εἰς τέλος in the sense of "completely," and the Ep. of Barnabas, c. 16. § 8 (cited by Bretschneider): "Having received the forgiveness of our sins, and having placed our hope in the Name, we became new men, created again from the beginning" (πάλιν ἐξ ἀρχῆς).

ent expression, γεννηθῆναι ἐκ θεοῦ or ἐκ τοῦ θεοῦ, "to be born [or begotten] of God," which occurs once in the Gospel (i. 13) and nine times in the First Epistle, so that the presumption is that, if he had wished to convey that meaning here, he would have used here also that unambiguous expression.

But what is decisive as to the main point is the fact that Justin's word ἀναγεννηθῇ is actually substituted for γεννηθῇ ἄνωθεν in verse 3, or for the simple γεννηθῇ in verse 5, by a large number of Christian writers who unquestionably quote from John; so, besides the CLEMENTINE HOMILIES (xi. 26) and the CLEMENTINE EPITOME in both forms (c. 18), to which exception has been taken with no sufficient reason, IRENÆUS (Frag. 35, ed. Stieren, i. 846), EUSEBIUS (*In Isa.* i. 16, 17; Migne xxiv. 96), ATHANASIUS (*De Incarn.* c. 14), BASIL (*Adv. Eunom.* lib. v. Opp. i. 308 (437)), EPHRAEM SYRUS (*De Pœnit.* Opp. iii. 183 (ἀναγεννηθῇ ἄνωθεν)), CHRYSOSTOM (*In* I *Ep. ad Cor.* xv. 29, Opp. x. 378 (440)), CYRIL OF ALEXANDRIA (*In Joan.* iii. 5, ἐξαναγεννηθῇ δι' ὕδατος κ.τ.λ., so Pusey's critical ed., vol. i. p. 219; Aubert has γεννηθῇ ἐξ ὕδ.); and so, probably, ANASTASIUS SINAITA preserved in a Latin version (*Anagog. Contemp. in Hexaëm.* lib. iv., Migne lxxxix. 906, *regeneratus;* contra, col. 870 *genitus,* 916 *generatus*), and HESYCHIUS OF JERUSALEM in a Latin version (*In Levit.* xx. 9, Migne xciii. 1044, *regeneratus;* but col. 974, *renatus*). In the Old Latin version or versions and the Vulgate, the MSS. are divided in John iii. 3 between *natus* and *renatus,* and so in verse 4, 2d clause, between *nasci* and *renasci;* but in verse 5 *renatus fuerit* is the unquestionable reading of the Latin versions, presupposing, apparently, ἀναγεννηθῇ in the Greek. (See Tischendorf's 8th critical edition of the Greek Test. *in loc.*) The Latin Fathers, with the exception of Tertullian and Cyprian, who have both readings, and of the author *De Rebaptismate* (c. 3), in quoting the passage, almost invariably have *renatus.*

We occasionally find ἀναγεννηθῆναι, "to be born again," for γεννηθῆναι, "to be born," in the first clause of verse 4; so EPHRAEM SYRUS (*De Pœnit.* Opp. iii. 183), and CYRIL OF ALEXANDRIA (*Glaph. in Exod.* lib. iii. Opp. i. a. 341).

From all that has been said, it will be seen that the use of ἀναγεννηθῆτε here by Justin is easily explained. Whether ἄνωθεν in John really means "from above" or "anew" is of little importance in its bearing on our question: there can be no doubt that Justin *may* have understood it in the latter sense; and, even if he did not, the use of the term ἀναγεννᾶσθαι here was very natural, as is shown by the way in which the passage is quoted by Irenæus, Eusebius, and many other writers cited above.

4. The next variation, the change of "*cannot* see" or "enter into" (οὐ δύναται ἰδεῖν or εἰσελθεῖν εἰς, *Lat.* non potest videre, *or* intrare *or* introire in), into "*shall* not" or "*shall in no wise* see" or "enter into" (οὐ μὴ ἴδῃ, once ἴδοι, or οὐ μὴ εἰσέλθῃ or εἰσέλθητε εἰς, once οὐκ εἰσελεύσεται εἰς, *Lat.* non videbit, *or* intrabit *or* introibit in), is both so natural (comp. Matt. xviii. 3) and so trivial as hardly to deserve mention. It is perhaps enough to say that I have noted *sixty-nine* examples of it in the quotations of this passage by *forty-two* different writers among the Greek and Latin Fathers. It is to be observed that in most of the quotations of the passage by the Fathers, verses 3 and 5 are mixed in different ways, as might be expected.

5. The change of "kingdom of *God*" into "kingdom of *heaven*" is perfectly natural, as they are synonymous expressions, and as the phrase "kingdom of heaven" is used in the passage of Matthew already referred to, the language of which was likely to be more or less confounded in recollection with that of this passage in John. The change is actually made in several Greek MSS. in the 5th verse of John, including the Sinaitic, and is even received by Tischendorf into the text, though, I believe, on insufficient grounds. But a great number of Christian writers in quoting from John make just the same change; so the DOCETIST in HIPPOLYTUS (*Ref. Hær.* viii. 10, p. 267), the CLEMENTINE HOMILIES (xi. 26), the RECOGNITIONS (i. 69; vi. 9), the CLEMENTINE EPITOME (c. 18) in both forms, IRENÆUS (Frag. 35, ed. Stieren), ORIGEN in a Latin version twice (*Opp.* iii. 948; iv. 483), the APOSTOLICAL CONSTITUTIONS (vi. 15), EUSEBIUS twice (*In Isa.* i. 16, 17; iii. 1, 2; Migne xxiv. 96, 109), PSEUD-ATHANASIUS (*Quæst. ad Antioch.* 101, Opp. ii. 291),

EPHRAEM SYRUS (*De Pœnit.* Opp. iii. 183), CHRYSOSTOM five times (*Opp.* iv. 681 (789); viii. 143 ᵈᵉ (165), 144ᵈ (165), 144ᵇ (166)), THEODORET (*Quæst. in Num.* 35, Migne lxxx. 385), BASIL OF SELEUCIA (*Orat.* xxviii. 3), ANASTASIUS SINAITA in a Latin version three times (Migne lxxxix. 870, 906, 916), HESYCHIUS OF JERUSALEM in a Latin version twice (Migne xciii. 974, 1044), THEODORUS ABUCARA (*Opuscc.* c. 17, Migne xcvii. 1541), TERTULLIAN (*De Bapt.* c. 13), ANON. *De Rebaptismate* (c. 3), PHILASTRIUS (*Hær.* 120 and 148, ed. Oehler), CHROMATIUS (*In Matt.* iii. 14, Migne xx. 329), JEROME twice (*Ep.* 69, al. 83, and *In Isa.* i. 16; Migne xxii. 660, xxv. 35), AUGUSTINE seven times (*Opp.* ii. 1360, 1361; v. 1745; vi. 327; vii. 528; ix. 630; x. 207, ed. Bened. 2da), and a host of other Latin Fathers.

It should be observed that many of the writers whom I have cited *combine* three or four of these variations from John. It may be well to give, further, some additional illustrations of the freedom with which this passage is sometimes quoted and combined with others. One example has already been given from Clement of Alexandria. (See No. 2.) TERTULLIAN (*De Bapt.* 12) quotes it thus: "The Lord says, Except a man shall be born of water, he *hath not life*,"—Nisi natus ex aqua quis erit, non *habet vitam*. Similarly ODO CLUNIACENSIS (*Mor. in Job.* iii. 4, Migne cxxxiii. 135): "Veritas autem dicit, Nisi quis *renatus* fuerit ex aqua et Spiritu sancto, non *habet vitam æternam.*" ANASTASIUS SINAITA, as preserved in a Latin version (*Anagog. Contempl. in Hexaëm.* lib. v., Migne lxxxix. 916), quotes the passage as follows: "dicens, Nisi quis fuerit generatus ex aqua et Spiritu *qui fertur super aquam,* non *intrabit in* regnum *cælorum.*" The APOSTOLICAL CONSTITUTIONS (vi. 15) as edited by Cotelier and Ueltzen read: "For the Lord saith, Except a man be *baptized* with ($\beta\alpha\pi\tau\iota\sigma\theta\hat{\eta}$ $\dot{\epsilon}\xi$) water and the Spirit, he *shall in no wise* enter into the kingdom of *heaven.*" Here, indeed, Lagarde, with two MSS., edits $\gamma\epsilon\nu\nu\eta\theta\hat{\eta}$ for $\beta\alpha\pi\tau\iota\sigma\theta\hat{\eta}$, but the more difficult reading may well be genuine. Compare EUTHYMIUS ZIGABENUS (*Panopl.* pars ii. tit. 23, Adv. Bogomilos, c 16, in the Latin version in Max. Bibl. Patrum, xix.

224), "Nisi quis *baptizatus* fuerit ex aqua et Spiritu *sancto*, non *intrabit in* regnum Dei," and see Jeremy Taylor, as quoted below. DIDYMUS OF ALEXANDRIA gives as the words of Christ (εἶπεν δέ), "Ye must be born *of water*" (*De Trin.* ii. 12, p. 250, Migne xxxix. 672). It will be seen that all these examples purport to be express quotations.

My principal object in this long discussion has been to show how false is the assumption on which the author of *Supernatural Religion* proceeds in his treatment of Justin's quotations, and those of other early Christian writers. But the fallacy of his procedure may, perhaps, be made more striking by some illustrations of the way in which the very passage of John which we have been considering is quoted by a modern English writer. I have noted nine quotations of the passage by Jeremy Taylor, who is not generally supposed to have used many apocryphal Gospels. All of these differ from the common English version, and only two of them are alike. They exemplify *all* the peculiarities of variation from the common text upon which the writers of the Tübingen school and others have laid such stress as proving that Justin cannot have here quoted John. I will number these quotations, with a reference to the volume and page in which they occur in Heber's edition of Jeremy Taylor's Works, London, 1828, 15 vols. 8vo, giving also such specifications as may enable one to find the passages in any other edition of his complete Works; and, without copying them all in full, will state their peculiarities. No. 1. Life of Christ, Part I. Sect. IX. Disc. VI. Of Baptism, part i. § 12. Heber, vol. ii. p. 240.— No. 2. *Ibid.* Disc. VI. Of baptizing Infants, part ii. § 26. Heber, ii. 288.— No. 3. *Ibid.* § 32. Heber, ii. 292.— No. 4. Liberty of Prophesying, Sect. XVIII. § 7. Heber, viii. 153.— No. 5. *Ibid.* Ad 7. Heber, viii. 190.— No. 6. *Ibid.* Ad 18. Heber, viii. 191.— No. 7. *Ibid.* Ad 18. Heber, viii. 193.— No. 8. Disc. of Confirm. Sect. I. Heber, xi. 238.— No. 9. *Ibid.* Heber, xi. 244.

We may notice the following points:—

1. He has "unless" for "except," uniformly. This is a trifling variation; but, reasoning after the fashion of *Super-*

natural Religion, we should say that this uniformity of variation could not be referred to accident, but proved that he quoted from a different text from that of the authorized version.

2. He has "kingdom of *heaven*" for "kingdom of *God*" six times; viz., Nos. 1, 2, 3, 4, 5, 7.

3. "*Heaven*" simply for "kingdom of God" once; No. 6.

4. "*Shall not* enter" for "*cannot* enter" four times; Nos. 4, 5, 7, 8; comp. also No. 6.

5. The second person plural, *ye*, for the third person singular, twice; Nos. 3, 7.

6. "*Baptized with* water" for "*born of* water" once; No. 7.

7. "Born *again by* water" for "born *of* water" once; No. 6.

8. "*Both of* water and the Spirit" for "*of* water and *of* the Spirit" once; No. 9.

9. "Of" is *omitted* before "the Spirit" six times; Nos. 1, 2, 3, 6, 7, 8.

10. "Holy" is *inserted* before "Spirit" twice; Nos. 1, 8.

No. 1 reads, for example, "*Unless* a man be born of water and the *Holy* Spirit, he cannot enter into the kingdom of heaven."

Supernatural Religion insists that, when Justin uses such an expression as "Christ said," we may expect a verbally accurate quotation.* Now nothing is more certain than that the Christian Fathers frequently use such a formula when they mean to give merely the substance of what Christ said, and not the exact words; but let us apply our author's principle to Jeremy Taylor. No. 3 of his quotations reads thus:

"Therefore our Lord hath defined it, *Unless ye* be born of water and the Spirit, *ye* cannot enter into the kingdom of heaven."

No. 6 reads, "Though Christ said, *None but those that are born again by* water and the Spirit *shall* enter into *heaven*."

No. 7 reads, "For Christ never said, *Unless ye be baptized*

---

* "Justin, in giving the words of Jesus, clearly professed to make an exact quotation."—*Supernatural Religion*, ii. 309, 7th ed.

with fire and the Spirit, *ye shall not* enter into the kingdom of *heaven*, but of water and the Spirit he *did say it*."

I will add one quotation from the Book of Common Prayer, which certainly must be quoting from another apocryphal Gospel, different from those used by Jeremy Taylor (he evidently had several), inasmuch as it professes to give the very words of Christ, and gives them *twice* in precisely the same form:—

"Our Saviour Christ saith, *None can* enter into the kingdom of God except he be *regenerate and* born *anew* of water and of the *Holy Ghost*." (*Public Baptism of Infants*, and *Baptism of those of Riper Years*.)

It has been shown, I trust, that in this quotation of the language of Christ respecting regeneration the verbal differences between Justin and John are not such as to render it improbable that the former borrowed from the latter. The variations of phraseology are easily accounted for, and are matched by similar variations in writers who unquestionably used the Gospel of John.

The positive reasons for believing that Justin derived his quotation from this source are, (1) the fact that in no other report of the teaching of Christ except that of John do we find this figure of the new birth; (2) the insistence in both Justin and John on the necessity of the new birth to an entrance into the kingdom of heaven; (3) its mention in both in connection with baptism; (4) and last and most important of all, the fact that Justin's remark on the impossibility of a second natural birth is such a platitude in the form in which he presents it, that we cannot regard it as original. We can only explain its introduction by supposing that the language of Christ which he quotes was strongly associated in his memory with the question of Nicodemus as recorded by John.* Other evidences of the use of the Fourth Gospel by Justin are the following:—

(*a*) While Justin's conceptions in regard to the Logos were undoubtedly greatly affected by Philo and the Alexandrian

---

* Engelhardt in his recent work on Justin observes: "This remark sets aside all doubt of the reference to the fourth Gospel."—*Das Christenthum Justins des Märtyrers*, Erlangen, 1878,

philosophy, the doctrine of the *incarnation* of the Logos was utterly foreign to that philosophy, and could only have been derived, it would seem, from the Gospel of John. He accordingly speaks very often in language similar to that of John (i. 14) of the Logos as "made flesh," * or as "having become man." † That in the last phrase he should prefer the term "man" to the Hebraistic "flesh" can excite no surprise. With reference to the deity of the Logos and his instrumental agency in creation, compare also especially *Apol.* ii. 6, "through him God created all things" (δι' αὐτοῦ πάντα ἔκτισε), *Dial.* c. 56, and *Apol.* i. 63, with John i. 1–3. Since the Fathers who immediately followed Justin, as Theophilus, Irenæus, Clement, Tertullian, unquestionably founded their doctrine of the incarnation of the Logos on the Gospel of John, the presumption is that Justin did the same. He professes to hold his view, in which he owns that some Chris-

---

p. 350. Weizsäcker is equally strong.—*Untersuchungen über die evang. Geschichte*, Gotha, 1864, pp. 228, 229.

Dr. Edwin A. Abbott, in the very interesting article *Gospels* in vol. x. of the ninth edition of the Encyclopædia Britannica, objects that Justin cannot have quoted the Fourth Gospel here, because "he is arguing for baptism by *water*," and "it is inconceivable that . . . he should not only quote inaccurately, but omit the very words [John iii. 5] that were best adapted to support his argument." (p. 821.) But Justin is not addressing an "argument" to the Roman Emperor and Senate for the necessity of baptism by water, but simply giving an account of Christian rites and Christian worship. And it is not the mere rite of baptism by water as such, but the necessity of the new birth through repentance and a voluntary change of life on the part of him who dedicates himself to God by this rite, on which Justin lays the main stress,—"the baptism of the soul from wrath and covetousness, envy and hatred." (Comp. *Dial.* cc. 13, 14, 18.) Moreover, the simple word ἀναγεννηθῆτε, as he uses it in the immediate context, and as it was often used, includes the idea of baptism. This fact alone answers the objection. A perusal of the chapter in which Justin treats the subject (*Apol.* i. 61) will show that it was not at all necessary to his purpose in quoting the words of Christ to introduce the ἐξ ὕδατος. It would almost seem as if Dr. Abbott must have been thinking of the Clementine Homilies (xi. 24–27; xiii. 21), where excessive importance *is* attached to the mere element of water.

* σαρκοποιηθείς; *e.g.*, *Apol.* c. 32, ὁ λόγος, ὃς τίνα τρόπον σαρκοποιηθεὶς ἄνθρωπος γέγονεν. So c. 66 *bis*; *Dial.* cc. 45, 84, 87, 100. Comp. *Dial.* cc. 48 ("was born a man of like nature with us, having flesh"), 70 ("became embodied").

† ἄνθρωπος γενόμενος; *Apol.* i. cc. 5 ("the Logos himself who took form and became man"), 23 *bis*, 32, 42, 50, 53, 63 *bis*; *Apol.* ii. c. 13; *Dial.* cc. 48, 57, 64, 67, 68 *bis*, 76, 85, 100, 101, 125 *bis*. I have availed myself in this and the preceding note of the references given by Professor Drummond in his article "Justin Martyr and the Fourth Gospel," in the *Theol. Review* for April and July, 1877; see vol. xiv., p. 172. To this valuable essay I am much indebted, and shall have occasion to refer to it repeatedly. Professor Drummond compares at length Justin's doctrine of the Logos with that of the proem to the Fourth Gospel, and decides rightly, I think, that the statement of the former "is, beyond all question, in a more developed form" than that of the latter. In John it is important to observe that λόγος is used with a meaning derived from the sense of "word" rather than "reason," as in Philo and Justin. The subject is too large to be entered upon here.

tians do not agree with him, "because we have been commanded by Christ himself not to follow the doctrines of men, but those which were proclaimed by the blessed prophets and *taught by* HIM." (*Dial.* c. 48.) Now, as Canon Westcott observes, "the Synoptists do not anywhere declare Christ's pre-existence."* And where could Justin suppose himself to have found this doctrine taught by Christ except in the Fourth Gospel? Compare *Apol.* i. 46: "That Christ is the first-born of God, being the Logos [the divine Reason] of which every race of men have been partakers [comp. John i. 4, 5, 9], we *have been taught* and have declared before. And those who have lived according to Reason are Christians, even though they were deemed atheists; as, for example, Socrates and Heraclitus and those like them among the Greeks."

(*b*) But more may be said. In one place (*Dial.* c. 105) Justin, according to the natural construction of his language and the course of his argument, appears to refer to the "Memoirs" as the source from which he and other Christians had learnt that Christ as the Logos was the "only-begotten" Son of God, a title applied to him by John alone among the New Testament writers; see John i. 14, 18; iii. 16, 18. The passage reads, "For that he was the only-begotten of the Father of the universe, having been begotten by him in a peculiar manner as his Logos and Power, and having afterwards become man through the virgin, as we have learned from the Memoirs, I showed before." It is *possible* that the clause, "as we have learned from the Memoirs," refers not to the main proposition of the sentence, but only to the fact of the birth from a virgin; but the context as well as the natural construction leads to a different view, as Professor Drummond has ably shown in the article in the *Theological Review* (xiv. 178–182) already referred to in a note. He observes:—

"The passage is part of a very long comparison, which Justin institutes between the twenty-second Psalm and the recorded events of

---

*"Introd. to the Gospel of St. John," in *The Holy Bible . . . with . . . Commentary,* etc., ed. by F. C. Cook, *N.T.* vol. ii. (1880), p. lxxxiv.

Christ's life. For the purposes of this comparison he refers to or quotes "the Gospel" once, and "the Memoirs" ten times, and further refers to the latter three times in the observations which immediately follow. . . . They are appealed to here because they furnish the successive steps of the proof by which the Psalm is shown to be prophetic."

In this case the words in the Psalm (xxii. 20, 21) which have to be illustrated are, "Deliver my soul from the sword, and my only-begotten [Justin perhaps read "*thy* only-begotten"] from the power of the dog. Save me from the mouth of the lion, and my humiliation from the horns of unicorns." "These words," Justin remarks, "are again in a similar manner a teaching and prophecy of the things that belonged to him [τῶν ὄντων αὐτῷ] and that were going to happen. FOR that he was the only-begotten," etc., as quoted above. Professor Drummond well observes : —

"There is here no ground of comparison whatever except in the word μονογενής [" only-begotten "]. . . . It is evident that Justin understood this as referring to Christ; and accordingly he places the same word emphatically at the beginning of the sentence in which he proves the reference of this part of the Psalm to Jesus. For the same reason he refers not only to events, but to τὰ ὄντα αὐτῷ [" the things that belonged to him "]. These are taken up first in the nature and title of μονογενής, which immediately suggests λόγος and δύναμις [" Logos " and "power "], while the events are introduced and discussed afterwards. The allusion here to the birth through the virgin has nothing to do with the quotation from the Old Testament, and is probably introduced simply to show how Christ, although the only-begotten Logos, was nevertheless a man. If the argument were, — These words allude to Christ, because the Memoirs tell us that he was born from a virgin, — it would be utterly incoherent. If it were, — These words allude to Christ, because the Memoirs say that he was the only-begotten, — it would be perfectly valid from Justin's point of view. It would not, however, be suitable for a Jew, for whom the fact that Christ was μονογενής, not being an historical event, had to rest upon other authority; and therefore Justin changing his usual form, says that he had already explained to him a doctrine which the Christians learned from the Memoirs. It appears to me, then, most probable, that the peculiar Johannine title μονογενής existed in the Gospels used by Justin. *

In what follows, Prof. Drummond answers Thoma's ob-

---

* Justin also designates Christ as "the only-begotten Son" in a fragment of his work against Marcion, preserved by Irenæus, *Hær.* iv. 6. § 2. Comp. Justin, *Apol.* i. c. 23 ; ii. c. 6; *Dial.* c. 48.

jections * to this view of the passage, correcting some mistranslations. In the expression, "as I showed before," the reference may be, not to c. 100, but to c. 61 and similar passages, where it is argued that the Logos was "begotten by God before all creatures," which implies a unique generation.

(*c*) In the Dialogue with Trypho (c. 88), Justin cites as the words of John the Baptist: "I am not the Christ, but the voice of one crying"; οὐκ εἰμὶ ὁ Χριστός, ἀλλὰ φωνὴ βοῶντος. This declaration, "I am not the Christ," and this application to himself of the language of Isaiah, are attributed to the Baptist only in the Gospel of John (i. 20, 23; comp. iii. 28). Hilgenfeld recognizes here the use of this Gospel.

(*d*) Justin says of the Jews, "They are justly upbraided ... by Christ himself as knowing neither the Father nor the Son" (*Apol.* i. 63). Comp. John viii. 19, "Ye neither know me nor my Father"; and xvi. 3, "They have not known the Father nor me." It is true that Justin quotes in this connection Matt. xi. 27; but his language seems to be influenced by the passages in John above cited, in which alone the Jews are directly addressed.

(*e*) Justin says that "Christ healed those who were blind from their birth," τοὺς ἐκ γενετῆς πηρούς (*Dial.* c. 49; comp. *Apol.* i. 22, ἐκ γενετῆς πονηρούς, where several editors, though not Otto, would substitute πηρούς by conjecture). There seems to be a reference here to John ix. 1, where we have τυφλὸν ἐκ γενετῆς, the phrase ἐκ γενετῆς, "from birth," being peculiar to John among the Evangelists, and πηρός being a common synonyme of τυφλός; comp. the Apostolical Constitutions v. 7. § 17, where we have ὁ ἐκ γενετῆς πηρός in a clear reference

---

*In Hilgenfeld's *Zeitschrift für wiss. Theol.*, 1875, xviii. 551 ff. For other discussions of this passage, one may see Semisch, *Die apost. Denkwürdigkeiten* u.s.w., p. 188 f.; Hilgenfeld, *Krit. Untersuchungen* u.s.w., p. 300 f. (*versus* Semisch); Riggenbach, *Die Zeugnisse f. d. Ev. Johannis*, Basel, 1866, p. 163 f.; Tischendorf, *Wann wurden unsere Evangelien verfasst?* p. 32, 4e Aufl. But Professor Drummond's treatment of the question is the most thorough.

Grimm (*Theol. Stud. u. Krit.*, 1851, p. 687 ff.) agrees with Semisch that it is "in the highest degree arbitrary" to refer Justin's expression, "as we have learned from the Memoirs," merely to the participial clause which mentions the birth from a virgin; but like Thoma, who agrees with him that the reference is to the designation "only-begotten," he thinks that Justin has in mind merely the confession of Peter (Matt. xvi. 16), referred to in *Dial.* c. 100. This rests on the false assumption that Justin can only be referring back to c. 100, and makes him argue that "the Son" merely is equivalent to "the only-begotten Son."

to this passage of John, and the Clementine Homilies xix. 22, where περὶ τοῦ ἐκ γενετῆς πηροῦ occurs also in a similar reference.* John is the only Evangelist who mentions the healing of any congenital infirmity.

(*f*) The exact coincidence between Justin (*Apol.* i. 52; comp. *Dial.* cc. 14 (quoted as from *Hosea*), 32, 64, 118) and John (xix. 37) in citing Zechariah xii. 10 in a form different from the Septuagint, ὄψονται εἰς ὃν ἐξεκέντησαν, "they shall look on him whom they pierced," instead of ἐπιβλέψονται πρὸς μὲ ἀνθ' ὧν κατωρχήσαντο, is remarkable, and not sufficiently explained by supposing both to have borrowed from Rev. i. 7, "every eye shall see him, and they who pierced him." Much stress has been laid on this coincidence by Semisch (p. 200 ff.) and Tischendorf (p. 34); but it is possible, if not rather probable, that Justin and John have independently followed a reading of the Septuagint which had already attained currency in the first century as a correction of the text in conformity with the Hebrew.†

(*g*) Compare *Apol.* i. 13 (cited by Prof. Drummond, p. 323), "Jesus Christ who became our teacher of these things and *was born to this end* (εἰς τοῦτο γεννηθέντα), who was crucified under Pontius Pilate," with Christ's answer to Pilate (John xviii. 37), "To this end have I been born, εἰς τοῦτο γεγέννημαι, . . . that I might bear witness to the truth."

(*h*) Justin says (*Dial.* c. 56, p. 276 D), "I affirm that he never did or spake any thing but what he that made the world, above whom there is no other God, willed that he should both do and speak"; ‡ comp. John viii. 28, 29: "As

---

*The context in Justin, as Otto justly remarks, proves that πηροὺς must here signify "blind," not "maimed"; comp. the quotation from Isa. xxxv. 5, which precedes, and the "causing this one to see," which follows. Keim's exclamation — "not a blind man at all!" — would have been spared, if he had attended to this. (See his *Gesch. Jesu von Nazara*, i. 139, note; i. 189, Eng. trans.)

† See Credner, *Beiträge* u.s.w., ii. 293 ff.

‡ Dr. Davidson (*Introd. to the Study of the N.T.*, London, 1868, ii. 370) translates the last clause, "intended that he should do and *to associate with*" (sic). Though the meaning "to converse with," and then "to speak," "to say," is not assigned to ὁμιλεῖν in Liddell and Scott, or Rost and Palm's edition of Passow, Justin in the very next sentence uses λαλεῖν as an equivalent substitute, and this meaning is common in the later Greek. See Sophocles, *Greek Lex.* s.v. ὁμιλέω. Of Dr. Davidson's translation I must confess my inability to make either grammar or sense.

the Father taught me, I speak these things; and ... I always do the things that please him"; also John iv. 34; v. 19, 30; vii. 16; xii. 49, 50. In the language of Trypho which immediately follows (p. 277 A), "We do not suppose that you represent him to have *said* or done or *spoken* anything contrary to the will of the Creator of the universe," we are particularly reminded of John xii. 49, — "The Father who sent me hath himself given me a commandment, what I should *say* and what I should *speak*."

(*i*) Referring to a passage of the Old Testament as signifying that Christ "was to rise from the dead on the third day after his crucifixion," Justin subjoins (*Dial.* c. 100), "which he received from his Father," or more literally, "which [thing] he has, having received it from his Father," ὃ ἀπὸ τοῦ πατρὸς λαβὼν ἔχει. A reference here to John x. 18 seems probable, where Jesus says respecting his life, "I have authority (ἐξουσίαν) to lay it down, and I have authority to receive it again (πάλιν λαβεῖν αὐτήν); this charge I received from my Father" (ἔλαβον παρὰ τοῦ πατρός μου).

(*k*) Justin says, "We were taught that the bread and wine were the flesh and blood of that Jesus who was made flesh." (*Apol.* i. c. 66.) This use of the term "flesh" instead of "body" in describing the bread of the Eucharist suggests John vi. 51-56.

(*l*) Professor Drummond notes that Justin, like John (iii. 14, 15), regards the elevation of the brazen serpent in the wilderness as typical of the crucifixion (*Apol.* i. c. 60; *Dial.* cc. 91, 94, 131), and in speaking of it says that it denoted "salvation to those who flee for refuge to him who sent his crucified Son into the world" (*Dial.* c. 91).* "Now this idea of God's sending his Son into the world occurs in the same connection in John iii. 17, and strange as it may appear, it is an idea which in the New Testament is peculiar to John." Prof. Drummond further observes that "in the four instances in which John speaks of Christ as being sent into the world, he prefers ἀποστέλλω, so that Justin's phrase is

---

* Or, as it is expressed in *Dial.* c. 94, "salvation to those *who believe in him* who was to die through this sign, the cross," which comes nearer to John iii. 15.

not entirely coincident with the Johannine. But the use of πέμπω ["to send"] itself is curious. Except by John, it is applied to Christ in the New Testament only twice, whereas John uses it [thus] twenty-five times. Justin's language, therefore, in the thought which it expresses, in the selection of words, and in its connection, is closely related to John's, and has no other parallel in the New Testament." (*Theol. Rev.* xiv. 324.) Compare also *Dial.* c. 140, "according to the will of the Father who sent him," etc., and *Dial.* c. 17, "the only blameless and righteous Light sent from God to men."

(*m*) Lücke, Otto, Semisch, Keim, Mangold, and Drummond are disposed to find a reminiscence of John i. 13 in Justin's language where, after quoting from Genesis xlix. 11, he says, "since his blood was not begotten of human seed, but by the will of God" (*Dial.* c. 63; comp. the similar language *Apol.* i. 32; *Dial.* cc. 54, "by the power of God"; 76). They suppose that Justin referred John i. 13 to Christ, following an early reading of the passage, namely, ὅς... ἐγεννήθη, "who *was* born" [*or* "begotten"] instead of "who *were* born." We find this reading in Irenæus (*Hær.* iii. 16. § 2; 19. § 2), Tertullian (*De Carne Christi* cc. 19, 24), Ambrose once, Augustine once, also in Codex Veronensis (b) of the Old Latin, and some other authorities. Tertullian indeed boldly charges the Valentinians with corrupting the text by changing the singular to the plural. Rönsch, whom no one will call an "apologist," remarks, "The citation of these words ... certainly belongs to the proofs that Justin Martyr knew the Gospel of John."* I have noticed this, in deference to these authorities, but am not confident that there is any reference in Justin's language to John i. 13.

(*n*) Justin says (*Dial.* c. 88), "The *Apostles* have written" that at the baptism of Jesus "as he came up from the water the Holy Spirit as a dove lighted upon him." The descent of the Holy Spirit as a dove is mentioned by the Apostles Matthew and John (Matt. iii. 16; John i. 32, 33). This is

---

* *Das neue Testament Tertullians*, Leipz. 1871, p. 654.

the only place in which Justin uses the expression "the Apostles have written."

(*o*) Justin says (*Dial.* c. 103) that Pilate sent Jesus to Herod *bound*. The binding is not mentioned by Luke; but if Justin used the Gospel of John, the mistake is easily explained through a confusion in memory of Luke xxiii. 7 with John xviii. 24 (comp. ver. 12); and this seems the most natural explanation; see however Matt. xxvii. 2; Mark xv. 1. Examples of such a confusion of different passages repeatedly occur in Justin's quotations from the Old Testament, as also of his citing the Old Testament for facts which it does not contain.*

(*p*) The remark of Justin that the Jews dared to call Jesus a magician (comp. Matt. ix. 34; xii. 24) and *a deceiver of the people* (λαόπλανον) reminds one strongly of John vii. 12; see however also Matt. xxvii. 63. — "Through his stripes," says Justin (*Dial.* c. 17), "there is healing to those who through him come to the Father," which suggests John xiv. 6, "No man cometh to the Father but through me"; but the reference is uncertain; comp. Eph. ii. 18, and Heb. vii. 25 with the similar expression in *Dial.* c. 43. — So also it is not clear that in the προσκυνοῦμεν, λόγῳ καὶ ἀληθείᾳ τιμῶντες (*Apol.* i. 6) there is any allusion to John iv. 24. † — I pass over sundry passages where Bindemann, Otto, Semisch, Thoma, Drummond and others have found resemblances more or less striking between the language of Justin and

---

*See, for example, *Apol.* i. 44, where the words in Deut. xxx. 15, 19, are represented as addressed to *Adam* (comp. Gen. ii. 16, 17); and *Apol.* i. 60, where Justin refers to Num. xxi. 8, 9 for various particulars found only in his own imagination. The extraordinary looseness with which he quotes Plato here (as elsewhere) may also be noted (see the *Timæus* c. 12, p. 36 B, C). On Justin's quotations from the Old Testament, which are largely marked by the same characteristics as his quotations from the Gospels, see Credner, *Beiträge* u.s.w., vol. ii. (1838); Norton, *Genuineness* etc., i. 213 ff., and Addit. Notes, p. ccxviii. ff., 2d ed., 1846 (1st ed. 1837); Semisch, *Die apost. Denkwürdigkeiten* u.s.w. (1848), p. 239 ff.; Hilgenfeld, *Krit. Untersuchungen* (1850), p. 46 ff.; Westcott, *Canon*, p. 121 ff., 172 ff., 4th ed. (1875); Sanday, *The Gospels in the Second Century* (1876), pp. 40 ff., 111 ff.

† Grimm, however, finds here "an unmistakable reminiscence" of John iv. 24. He thinks Justin used λόγῳ for πνεύματι and τιμῶντες for προσκυνοῦντες because πνεῦμα and προσκυνοῦμεν immediately precede. (*Theol. Stud. u. Krit.*, 1851, p. 691.) But λόγῳ καὶ ἀληθείᾳ seem to mean simply, "in accordance with reason and truth"; comp. *Apol.* i. 68, cited by Otto, also c. 13, μετὰ λόγου τιμῶμεν.

John, leaving them to the not very tender mercies of Zeller* and Hilgenfeld. †

(*q*) Justin's vindication of Christians for not keeping the Jewish Sabbath on the ground that "God has carried on the same administration of the universe during that day as during all others" (*Dial.* c. 29, comp. c. 23) is, as Mr. Norton observes, "a thought so remarkable, that there can be little doubt that he borrowed it from what was said by our Saviour when the Jews were enraged at his having performed a miracle on the Sabbath: — 'My Father has been working hitherto as I am working.'" — His argument also against the observance of the Jewish Sabbath from the fact that circumcision was permitted on that day may (*Dial.* c. 27) have been borrowed from John vii. 22, 23.

(*r*) I will notice particularly only one more passage, in which Professor Drummond proposes an original and very plausible explanation of a difficulty. In the larger Apology (c. 35), as he observes, the following words are quoted from Isaiah (lviii. 2), αἰτοῦσί με νῦν κρίσιν, "they now ask of me judgment"; and in evidence that this prophecy was fulfilled in Christ, Justin asserts, "they mocked him, and set him on the judgment-seat (ἐκάθισαν ἐπὶ βήματος), and said, Judge for us." This proceeding is nowhere recorded in our Gospels, but in John xix. 13 we read, "Pilate therefore brought Jesus out, and sat on the judgment-seat" (καὶ ἐκάθισεν ἐπὶ βήματος). But the words just quoted in the Greek, the correspondence of which with those of Justin will be noticed, admit in themselves the rendering, "and *set him* on the judgment-seat"; and what was more natural, as Prof. Drummond remarks, than that Justin, in his eagerness to find a fulfilment of the prophecy, should take them in this sense? "He might then add the statement that the people said κρῖνον ἡμῖν ['judge for us'] as an obvious inference from the fact of Christ's having been placed on the tribunal, just as in an earlier chapter (c. 32) he appends to the synoptic account the circum-

---

* *Die äusseren Zeugnisse . . . des vierten Evang.*, in the *Theol. Jahrbücher* (Tübingen) 1845, p. 600 ff.

† *Kritische Untersuchungen* u.s.w., p. 302 f.

stance that the ass on which Christ rode into Jerusalem was bound to a vine, in order to bring the event into connection with Genesis xlix. 11." (*Theol. Review*, xiv. 328.)

These evidences of Justin's use of the Gospel of John are strengthened somewhat by an indication, which has been generally overlooked, of his use of the First Epistle of John. In 1 John iii. 1 we read, according to the text now adopted by the best critics, as Lachmann, Tischendorf, Tregelles, Alford, Westcott and Hort, "Behold what love the Father hath bestowed upon us, that we should be called children of God; and we are so"; ἵνα τέκνα θεοῦ κληθῶμεν, καὶ ἐσμέν. This addition to the common text, καὶ ἐσμέν, "and we are," is supported by a great preponderance of external evidence. Compare now Justin (*Dial.* c. 123) : "We are both called true children of God, and we are so"; καὶ θεοῦ τέκνα ἀληθινὰ καλούμεθα καὶ ἐσμέν. The coincidence seems too remarkable to be accidental. Hilgenfeld takes the same view (*Einleit. in d. N. T.*, p. 69), and so Ewald (*Die johan. Schriften*, ii. 395, Anm. 4).

It also deserves to be considered that, as Justin wrote a work "Against all Heresies" (*Apol.* i. 26), among which he certainly included those of Valentinus and Basilides (*Dial.* c. 35), he could hardly have been ignorant of a book which, according to Irenæus, the Valentinians used *plenissime*, and to which the Basilidians and apparently Basilides himself also appealed (Hippol. *Ref. Hær.* vii. 22, 27). Credner recognizes the weight of this argument.* It can only be met by maintaining what is altogether improbable, that merely the *later* Valentinians and Basilidians made use of the Gospel, — a point which we shall examine hereafter.

In judging of the indications of Justin's use of the Fourth Gospel, the passages cited in addition to those which relate to his Logos doctrine will strike different persons differently. There will be few, however, I think, who will not feel that the one first discussed (that relating to the new birth) is in itself almost a decisive proof of such a use, and that the one relating to John the Baptist (*c*) is also strong. In regard to

---

* *Geschichte des neutest. Kanon* (1860), p. 15 f.; comp. pp. 9, 12.

not a few others, while the *possibility* of accidental agreement must be conceded, the probability is decidedly against this, and the accumulated probabilities form an argument of no little weight. It is not then, I believe, too much to say, that the strong presumption from the universal reception of our four Gospels as sacred books in the time of Irenæus that Justin's "Memoirs of Christ composed by Apostles and their companions" were the same books, is decidedly confirmed by these evidences of his use of the Fourth Gospel. We will next consider the further confirmation of this fact afforded by writers who flourished between the time of Justin and Irenæus, and then notice some objections to the view which has been presented.

The most weighty testimony is that of Tatian, the Assyrian, a disciple of Justin. His literary activity may be placed at about A.D. 155–170 (Lightfoot). In his "Address to the Greeks" he repeatedly quotes the Fourth Gospel, though without naming the author, in one case using the expression (τὸ εἰρημένον) which is several times employed in the New Testament (*e.g.* Acts ii. 16; Rom. iv. 18) in introducing a quotation from the Scriptures; see his *Orat. ad Græc.* c. 13, "And this then is that which hath been said, The darkness comprehendeth [*or* overcometh] not the light" (John i. 5); see also c. 19 (John i. 3); c. 4 (John iv. 24).* Still more important is the fact that he composed a Harmony of our Four Gospels which he called the *Diatessaron* (*i.e.* "the Gospel made out of Four"). This fact is attested by Eusebius (*Hist. Eccl.* iv. 29),† Epiphanius (*Hær.* xlvi. 1), who, however, writes from hearsay, and Theodoret, who in his work on Heresies (*Hær. Fab.* i. 20) says that he found more than two hundred copies of the book held in esteem in his diocese, and substituted for it copies of our Four Gospels.

---

* Even Zeller does not dispute that Tatian quotes the Fourth Gospel, and ascribed it to the Apostle John. (*Theol. Jahrb.* 1847, p. 158.)

† An expression used by Eusebius (οὐκ οἶδ' ὅπως, literally, "I know not how") has been misunderstood by many as implying that he had not seen the work; but Lightfoot has shown conclusively that this inference is wholly unwarranted. It only implies that the plan of the work seemed strange to him. See *Contemporary Review* for May, 1877, p. 1136, where Lightfoot cites 26 examples of this use of the phrase from the work of Origen against Celsus.

He tells us that Tatian, who is supposed to have prepared the Harmony after he became a Gnostic Encratite, had "cut away the genealogies and such other passages as show the Lord to have been born of the seed of David after the flesh." But notwithstanding this mutilation, the work seems to have been very popular in the orthodox churches of Syria as a convenient compendium. The celebrated Syrian Father, Ephraem, the deacon of Edessa, who died A.D. 373, wrote a commentary on it, according to Dionysius Bar-Salibi, who flourished in the last part of the twelfth century. Bar-Salibi was well acquainted with the work, citing it in his own Commentary on the Gospels, and distinguishing it from the Diatessaron of Ammonius, and from a later work by Elias Salamensis, also called Aphthonius. He mentions that it began with John i. 1 — "In the beginning was the Word." (See Assemani, *Biblioth. Orient.* ii. 158 ff.) Besides Ephraem, Aphraates, an earlier Syrian Father (A.D. 337) appears to have used it (*Hom.* i. p. 13 ed. Wright); and in the *Doctrine of Addai*, an apocryphal Syriac work, written probably not far from the middle of the third century, which purports to give an account of the early history of Christianity at Edessa, the people are represented as coming together "to the prayers of the service, and to [the reading of] the Old Testament and the New of the Diatessaron."* The *Doctrine of Addai* does not name the author of the *Diatessaron* thus read; but the facts already mentioned make the presumption strong that it was Tatian's. A scholion on Cod. 72 of the Gospels cites "Tatian's Gospel" for a remarkable reading of Matt. xxvii. 49 found in many ancient MSS.; and

---

*In Cureton's *Ancient Syriac Documents* (Lond. 1864) the text, published from a MS. in the British Museum, is here corrupt, reading *Ditonron*, a word without meaning; comp. Pratten's *Syriac Documents* (1871), p. 25, note, in the Ante-Nicene Christian Library, vol. xx. Cureton conjectured that the true reading was *Diatessaron* (see his note, p. 158), and his conjecture is confirmed by the St. Petersburg MS. published by Dr. George Phillips, *The Doctrine of Addai*, London, 1876; see his note, p. 34 f. Cureton's Syriac text (p. 15), as well as his translation (p. 15), reads *Ditonron*, not *Ditornon*, as Lightfoot, Pratten, and Phillips erroneously state, being misled by a misprint in Cureton's note. Phillips gives the reading correctly in the note to his Syriac text (p. 36). Moesinger, in the work described below, is also misled, spelling the word *Diathurnun* (Præf. p. iv). The difference between *Ditonron* and *Diatessaron* in the Syriac is very slight, affecting only a single letter.

it is also cited for a peculiar reading of Luke vii. 42.* So far the evidence is clear, consistent, and conclusive; but on the ground of a confusion between Tatian's Harmony and that of Ammonius on the part of a Syrian writer of the thirteenth century (Gregorius Abulpharagius or Bar-Hebræus), and of the two *persons* by a still later writer, Ebed-Jesu, both of which confusions can be traced to a misunderstanding of the language of Bar-Salibi, and for other reasons equally weak, † the fact that Tatian's work was a Harmony of our Four Gospels has been questioned by some German critics, and of course by *Supernatural Religion*. But the whole subject has been so thoroughly discussed and its obscurities so well cleared up by Bishop Lightfoot, in an article in the *Contemporary Review* for May, 1877, that the question may be regarded as settled. ‡ Lightfoot's view is confirmed by the recent publication of Ephraem's Commentary on the

---

*See Tischendorf, *N.T. Gr.* ed. 8va, on Matt. xxvii. 49, and Scholz, *N.T. Gr.*, vol. i., p. cxlix., and p. 243, note *x*.

† Such as that Victor of Capua (A.D. 545) says that it was called *Diapente* (*i.e.*, "made out of five"). But this is clearly a slip of the pen of Victor himself, or a mistake of some scribe; for, as Hilgenfeld (*Einleit.* p. 79, note) and Lightfoot remark, Victor is simply reporting *Eusebius's* account of it, and not only does Eusebius say that Tatian called it the *Diatessaron*, but Victor himself has just described it as "*unum ex quatuor.*" The strange mistake, for it can be nothing else, may possibly be accounted for by the fact that *Diatessaron* and *Diapente* being both musical terms, one might naturally recall the other, and lead to an unconscious substitution on the part of some absent-minded copyist. Under no circumstances can any inference about the composition of the work be drawn from this *Diapente*, for Victor derives his information from Eusebius, and not only do all the Greek MSS. in the passage referred to read *Diatessaron*, but this reading is confirmed by the very ancient, probably contemporary, Syriac version of Eusebius, preserved in a MS. of the sixth century, and by the Latin version of Rufinus, made a century and a half before Victor wrote. (See Lightfoot, p. 1143.) The mistake ascribed to the Syriac lexicographer Bar-Bahlul is proved to be due to an interpolator. (See Lightfoot, p. 1139, note.) The statement of Epiphanius, the most untrustworthy and blundering of the Fathers, that "it is called by some the Gospel according to the Hebrews" (*Hær.* xlvi. 1), if it had any foundation beyond a mere guess of the writer, may have originated from the omission of the genealogies, which were omitted also in one form of the Gospel according to the Hebrews (Epiph. *Hær.* xxx. 13, 14). The supposition that it *was* that Gospel contradicts all our information about the two works except the circumstance just mentioned; and that it had *additions* from that Gospel is a conjecture for which we have not a particle of evidence. (See Lightfoot, p. 1141; Lipsius in Smith and Wace's *Dict. of Christian Biog.* ii. 714.)

‡ To Lightfoot's article I am much indebted. The other writers who treat of the subject most fully are Credner, *Beiträge* u.s.w., i. 437-451, who has thrown more darkness upon it than anybody else; Daniel, *Tatianus der Apologet* (Halle, 1837), pp. 87-111, who has refuted Credner's arguments; Semisch, *Tatiani Diatessaron*, Vratisl. 1856; Hilgenfeld, *Einleit. in d. N.T.* (1875), pp. 75-79; *Supernatural Religion*, vol. ii., pp. 148-159, 7th ed.; and E. B. Nicholson, *The Gospel according to the Hebrews* (London, 1879), p. 16 f., and pp. 126-133, who does not appear to have seen Lightfoot's article, but exposes independently many of the errors and fallacies of *Supernatural Religion*. See also Norton, *Genuineness of the Gospels*, iii. 292 ff.

Diatessaron, to which I have already had occasion to refer.* This exists only in an Armenian version of the Syriac, made, it is supposed, in the fifth century. The Armenian text was published in the second volume of the collected Works of St. Ephraem in Armenian, printed at Venice in 1836 (4 vols. 8vo); but Aucher's Latin translation of the Commentary, revised and edited by G. Moesinger, who compared it with another Armenian manuscript, first appeared at Venice in 1876, and the work has hitherto been almost unnoticed by scholars.† It should be observed that Ephraem's commentary is only on select passages of the Harmony, unless the work which has come down to us is merely an abridgment. But there seems to be no ground for questioning the genuineness of the work ascribed to Ephraem; and little or no ground for doubting that the Harmony on which he is commenting is Tatian's, in accordance with the account of Dionysius Bar-Salibi. ‡ It agrees with what we know of Tatian's in omitting the genealogies and in beginning with the first verse of the Gospel of John. Further, the character of the text, so far as we can judge of it from a translation of a translation, is such as to lend confirmation to the view that it is Tatian's. It presents some very ancient various readings which accord remarkably with those of Justin Martyr and other early writers, and with the Curetonian Syriac where it differs from the later Peshito. ‖

---

* See Note A, no. 4.

† The volume is entitled: *Evangelii concordantis Expositio facta a Sancto Ephraemo Doctore Syro. In Latinum translata a R. P. Joanne Baptista Aucher Mechitarista cujus Versionem emendavit, Adnotationibus illustravit et edidit Dr. Georgius Moesinger.* Venetiis, Libraria PP. Mechitaristarum in Monasterio S. Lazari. 1876. 8vo. pp. xii., 292. Lipsius, art. *Gospels, Apocryphal*, in Smith and Wace's *Dict. of Christian Biog.*, vol. ii. (London, 1880), p. 713, is not even aware that the Armenian translation has been published.

‡ See Moesinger, *ubi supra*, Præf. p. ii. ff.

‖ We find, for example, the very ancient punctuation or construction which ends the sentence in John i. 3 with οὐδὲ ἕν, "not even one thing," connecting ὃ γέγονεν with ver. 4. (See Moesinger's edition, p. 5.) This accords with the citation of the passage by Tatian (*Orat. ad Græc.* c. 19). In Matt. i. 25, we read "sancte (*or* in sanctitate) habitabat cum ea" (Moesinger, pp. 23, 25, 26); so the Curetonian Syriac. In Matt. viii. 10 (p. 74), it reads, "*Non in aliquo* in Israël tantam fidem inveni," with Cod. Vaticanus (B), several of the best cursives, the MSS. a g¹. k q of the Old Latin, the Curetonian Syriac, Sahidic, Coptic, and Æthiopic versions, the Harclean Syriac in the margin, Augustine once, and the "*Opus Imperfectum*" on Matt. In Matt. xi. 27 (Moesinger, pp. 117, 216), it agrees with Justin, the Clementine Homilies, and the Gnostics in Irenæus, in the transposition of the clauses relating to the Father and the Son. (See

We may regard it then, I conceive, as an established fact that Tatian's *Diatessaron* was a Harmony of our four Gospels. So difficult and laborious a work would hardly have been undertaken, except to meet a want which had been widely felt. It implies that the four books used were recognized by those for whom it was intended as authoritative, and as possessing equal authority. Can we then believe that Tatian's Harmony represented a different set of books from the "Memoirs called Gospels" of his master Justin, which were read at the meetings for public worship in churches all over the Christian world as the authentic records of the life and teaching of Christ, the production of Apostles and their companions? Does not Tatian's unquestionable use of the Gospel of John in particular confirm the strong presumption from other facts that this Gospel was included in the "Memoirs" used by his master and by Christians generally twenty years before?

This presumption receives further confirmation from other testimonies to the existence and use of the Fourth Gospel between the time of Justin Martyr and Irenæus.

The treatise or fragment *On the Resurrection*, which Otto with many others ascribes to Justin, if not genuine, probably belongs to this period. In c. 1 we read, "The Logos of God, who was [*or* became] his Son, came to us clothed in flesh, revealing both himself and the Father, giving to us in himself the resurrection from the dead and the eternal life which follows." The allusions here to John i. 1, 14; xiv. 9; xi. 25, 26, seem unmistakable. So in c. 9, "He permitted them to handle him, and showed in his hands the marks of the nails," we have a reference to John xx. 25, 27, as well as to Luke xxiv. 39.

Melito, bishop of Sardis (*cir.* A.D. 165), in a fragment from

---

Note A, under no. 4.) In Matt. xix. 17, the text is given in Ephraem's commentary in different forms, but it seems to be, substantially, "Unus tantum est bonus, Pater (*or* Deus Pater) qui in cælis" (Moesinger, pp. 169, 170, 173); similarly, Justin Martyr once (*Dial.* c. 101), the Naassenes in Hippolytus (*Adv. Hær.* v. 7, p. 102), the Marcosians in Irenæus (*Hær.* i. 20. § 2), and the Clementine Homilies (xviii. 1, 3); see, for the numerous variations of reading here, Tischendorf's *N.T. Gr.* ed. 8va, *in loc.* Notice also the reading of John vii. 8 ("*Non* ascendo," Moesinger, p. 167); John iii. 13, quoted without the last clause of *text. recept.* (pp. 187, 189, comp. 168); John x. 8 (*ante me*, p. 200); Luke xxii. 44 ("et factus est sudor ejus ut guttæ sanguinis," p. 235; comp. Justin, *Dial.* c. 103).

his work on the Incarnation preserved by Anastasius Sinaita, speaks of Christ as "giving proof to us of his deity by signs [wrought] in the three years after his baptism, and of his humanity in the thirty years before his baptism." * This assignment of a duration of three years to his ministry must have been founded on the Gospel of John, which mentions three Passovers (ii. 13; vi. 4; xi. 55) besides the "feast of the Jews" referred to in John v. 1.

Claudius Apollinaris, bishop of Hierapolis in Phrygia (*cir.* A.D. 166), in a treatise on the Paschal Festival, refers to the apparent difference between John and the Synoptic Gospels as to the time of the death of Jesus. Apollinaris, relying on the Gospel of John, held that it was on the day on which the paschal lamb was killed, the 14th of Nisan; his opponents, appealing to the Gospel of Matthew, maintained that it was on the day following. Both Gospels were evidently received as authoritative by both parties.† He also refers in the same work to the piercing of the side of Jesus and the effusion of water and blood, mentioned only by John (xix. 34).‡

The Epistle of the Churches of Vienne and Lyons in Gaul to those of Asia and Phrygia, giving an account of their persecutions (A.D. 177), quotes the following as the words of the Lord: "There shall come a time in which whosoever killeth you shall think that he is offering a religious service to God," λατρείαν προσφέρειν τῷ θεῷ. The expression in the last clause is the same which is inadequately rendered in the common version "doeth God service" (John xvi. 2). ‖ The use of the word παράκλητος a little before in the Epistle, "having the

---

* See Anast. Sinait. *Hodeg.* or *Viæ Dux*, c. 13, in Migne, *Patrol. Gr.* lxxxix. col. 229, or Melito, Frag. vi. in Otto, *Corp. Apol. Christ.*, vol. ix. (1872), p. 416.

†*Chronicon Paschale*, vol. i., pp. 13, 14, ed. Dindorf; Apollinaris in Routh's *Rell. sacræ*, ed. alt. (1846), i. 160; or Otto, *Corp. Apol. Christ.*, ix. 486 f.

‡*Ibid.* p. 14, ed. Dindorf; Routh, *ibid.* p. 161; Otto, *ubi supra.* For a full view of the evidence of Melito and Apollinaris, and of the considerations which give it weight, see Lightfoot's article, "The Later School of St. John," in the *Contemporary Review* for February, 1876, xxvii. 471 ff.

‖ The letter is preserved in large part by Eusebius, *Hist. Eccl.* v. cc. 1-4. It may be consulted conveniently in Routh, *Rell. sacræ*, i. 295 ff., ed. alt. For the quotation, see *Epist.* c. 4; Routh, p. 300; Euseb. v. 1. § 15.

Paraclete within him," also suggests the Gospel of John; comp. John xiv. 16, 17.*

Athenagoras the Athenian (*cir.* A.D. 176), in his *Plea for Christians* addressed to M. Aurelius and Commodus, speaking of "the Logos of God the Father," says that "through him all things were made." (δι' αὐτοῦ πάντα ἐγένετο), the Father and the Son being one; and the Son being in the Father, and the Father in the Son"; language which seems evidently founded on John i. 3; x. 30, 38; xiv. 10, 11; xvii. 21, 22.†

Theophilus, bishop of Antioch A.D. 169–181, in his work in defence of Christianity addressed to Autolycus (A.D. 180), says, "The Holy Scriptures teach us, and all who were moved by the Spirit, among whom John says, 'In the beginning was the word [*or* Logos], and the Word was with God.'" He proceeds to quote John i. 3.‡

The Muratorian Canon (*cir.* A.D. 170), as has already been mentioned, ascribes the Gospel to the Apostle John, and gives an account of the circumstances under which it was written, fabulous doubtless in some of its details, but having probably a basis of truth. ‖

Celsus, the celebrated heathen adversary of Christianity (A.D. 178, Keim), professedly founds his statements concerning the history of Christ on "the writings of his disciples";** and his accounts are manifestly based on our four Gospels,††

---

* *Epist.* c. 3; Routh, p. 298; Euseb. v. 1. § 10. In the same section we have other expressions apparently borrowed from John xv. 13 and 1 John iii. 16. See, further, Lightfoot's article, "The Churches of Gaul," in the *Contemp. Review* for August, 1876, xxviii. 405 ff. An English translation of the Fragments of Melito and Apollinaris, and of the Epistle of the Churches of Vienne and Lyons, will be found appended to vol. ii. of Lactantius, in vol. xxii. of the Ante-Nicene Christian Library.

† *Suppl. pro Christ.* c. 10, p. 46, ed. Otto.

‡ *Ad Autol.* ii. 22, pp. 118–120, ed. Otto.

‖ See on this subject Lightfoot in the *Contemp. Review* for October, 1875, xxvi. 835 ff.; Matthew Arnold, *God and the Bible*, p. 248 (Eng. ed.); and Westcott, "Introd. to the Gospel of St. John," in *The Holy Bible . . . with . . . Commentary*, etc., ed. by F. C. Cook, *N.T.*, vol. ii. p. xxxv.

** Origen, *Cels.* ii. 13, 74; comp. 32, 53. He quotes these writings as possessing among Christians unquestioned authority: "We need," says he, "no other witness; for you fall upon your own swords" (ii. 74).

†† See fully in Lardner, *Testimonies of Ancient Heathens*, ch. xviii., *Works*, vii. 210–278; Kirchhofer, *Quellensammlung zur Gesch. des neutest. Canons* (1844), pp. 330–349; Keim, *Celsus' Wahres Wort* (1873), pp. 223–230. Comp. Norton, *Genuineness of the Gospels*, i. 142 ff.; E. A. Abbott, art. *Gospels*, in the *Encyc. Britannica*, 9th ed., x. 818.

though he does not name their authors. He refers to several circumstances peculiar to the narrative of John, as the blood which flowed from the body of Jesus at his crucifixion,* and the fact that Christ "after his death arose, and showed the marks of his punishment, and how his hands had been pierced." † He says that "some relate that one, and some that two angels came to the sepulchre, to announce that Jesus was risen." ‡ Matthew and Mark speak of but one angel, Luke and John mention two. He says that the Jews "challenged Jesus *in the temple* to produce some clear proof that he was the Son of God." ‖ He appears also to allude to the cry of Jesus, " I thirst," recorded only by John.** Referring to a declaration of Jesus, he satirically exclaims, "O Light and Truth!" designations of Christ characteristic of John's Gospel.†† He says that Jesus "after rising from the dead showed himself secretly to one woman only, and to his boon companions."‡‡ Here the first part of the statement seems to refer to John's account of the appearance of Christ to Mary Magdalene.

The heretical writings of this period clearly recognize the Fourth Gospel. Notwithstanding several apparent quotations or allusions, it was formerly maintained that the author of the Clementine Homilies could not possibly have used this Gospel, it being in such opposition to his opinions. But since the discovery of the Codex Ottobonianus, containing the missing portion of the book (first published by Dressel in his edition of the Homilies in 1853), there has been a change of view. That portion contains so clear a quotation of John ix. 1–3 (*Hom*. xix. 22) that Hilgenfeld has handsomely retracted his denial;‖‖ and, though Scholten and *Supernatu-*

---

*Origen, *Cels*. ii. 36, also i. 66; comp. John xix. 34.
†Origen, *Cels*. ii. 55, 59; John xx. 25, 27.
‡Origen, *Cels*. v. 52, 56; John xx. 12; comp. Luke xxiv. 4, 23.
‖Origen, *Cels*. i. 67; John ii. 18; comp. x. 23, 24. (Matt. xxi. 23.)
**Origen, *Cels*. ii. 37; John xix. 28.
††Origen, *Cels*. ii. 49; John viii. 12; ix. 5; xii. 46; xiv. 6.
‡‡Origen, *Cels*. ii. 70; John xx. 14–18. Compare, however, the Addition to Mark, xvi. 9.
‖‖*Einleit. in d. N.T.*, p. 43 f., note; comp. Matthew Arnold, *God and the Bible*, p. 277. Volkmar also recognizes the use of the Fourth Gospel here, but only as "an unapostolic *novum*"

ral Religion still resist the evidence, there can be little doubt about the final verdict of impartial criticism. Besides this passage and that about the new birth,* the Gospel of John seems to be used twice in *Hom.* iii. 52, once in a free quotation: "I am the gate of life; he that entereth in through me entereth into life, for there is no other teaching that can save" (comp. John x. 9, 10); and again, "My sheep hear my voice" (comp. John x. 27).

More important, and beyond any dispute, is the evidence of the use of the Fourth Gospel as the work of the Apostle John by the Gnostics of this period. Ptolemy, the disciple of Valentinus, in his Epistle to Flora, preserved by Epiphanius (*Hær.* xxxiii. 3), quotes John i. 3 as what "the Apostle says";† and, in the exposition of the Ptolemæo-Valentinian system given by Irenæus, a long passage is quoted from Ptolemy or one of his school in which he is represented as saying that "John, the disciple of the Lord, supposes a certain Beginning," etc., citing and commenting on John i. 1–5, 14, 18, in support of the Valentinian doctrine of the Ogdoad. ‡ The Valentinians, indeed, as we are told by Irenæus elsewhere, used the Gospel of John most abundantly (*Hær.* iii. 11. § 7). Heracleon, another disciple of Valentinus, wrote a commentary on it, large extracts from which are preserved by Origen. ‖ The book commonly cited as *Excerpta Theodoti* or *Doctrina Orientalis*, a compilation (with criticisms) from the writings of Theodotus and other Gnostics of the second century, ascribed to Clement of Alexandria and

---

(*Ursprung uns. Evv.*, 1866, p. 62 f., 134 f.). The question is well treated by Sanday, *The Gospels in the Second Century*, pp. 293 ff. It is to be observed that the incident of "*the* man blind from his birth" is introduced in the Homilies (xix. 22) as it is in the Apostolical Constitutions (v. 7. § 17) with the use of the definite article, as something well-known to the readers of the book. How does this happen, if the writer is taking it from "an unapostolic *novum*"? Drummond and Sanday have properly called attention to this use of the article.

* *Hom.* xi. 26; see pp. 29, 31.

† I follow the text of Dindorf in his edition of Epiphanius, vol. ii., pp. 199, 200, who reads τά τε πάντα for ἅτε πάντα and γεγονέναι οὐδέν for γέγονεν οὐδέν.

‡ Iren. *Hær.* i. 8. § 5. The old Latin version of Irenæus, which is often more trustworthy than the Greek as preserved by Epiphanius, ends the section referred to with the words: *Et Ptolemæus quidem ita.* For the Greek, generally, see Epiphanius, *Hær.* xxxi. 27, in Dindorf's edition, which gives the best text.

‖ These are collected in Grabe's *Spicilegium SS. Patrum*, etc., ii. 85–117, 237, ed. alt. (1714), and in Stieren's Irenæus, i. 938–971.

commonly printed with his works, contains many extracts from one or more writers of the Valentinian school, in which the Gospel of John is quoted and commented upon as the work of the Apostle. (See particularly cc. 6-8, also 3, 9, 13, 17-19, 26, 41, 45, 61, 62, 65, 73.)

The literature of the third quarter of the second century is fragmentary, but we have seen that it attests the use of the Fourth Gospel in the most widely separated regions of the Christian world, and by parties diametrically opposed in sentiment. The fact that this Gospel was used by those to whose opinions it was or seemed to be adverse — by the author of the Clementine Homilies, by Quartodecimans and their opponents, and especially by the Gnostics, who were obliged to wrest its language so violently to accommodate it to their systems — shows that to have won such a reception at that time it must have come down from an earlier period with commanding authority. Its use in Tatian's Diatessaron also makes this evident. It must have belonged to those "Memoirs" to which Justin appealed fifteen or twenty years before, and which were recognized by the Christians generally of his day as the authentic sources of information respecting the life and teaching of Christ. The particular evidence we have been examining, limited as it is by the scantiness of the literature, strengthens the general conclusion before drawn from the universal reception of our four Gospels in the time of Irenæus, and from the direct indications of the use of the Fourth Gospel by Justin. The evidence that this Gospel was one of his "Memoirs" is thus cumulative, and, unless it is countervailed by some very strong objections, must be regarded as decisive. Let us then consider the main objections which have been urged against this conclusion.

The first is that, according to *Supernatural Religion*, "The description which Justin gives of the manner of the teaching of Jesus excludes the idea that he knew the Fourth Gospel. 'Brief and concise were the sentences uttered by him: for he was no Sophist, but his word was the power of God.'

No one could for a moment assert that this applies to the long and artificial discourses of the Fourth Gospel." *

Here we may observe, in the first place, that Justin's Greek is not quite accurately translated. † The word rendered "sentences" is without the article; and Prof. Drummond translates the clause more correctly, "Brief and concise sayings have proceeded from him," remarking that "Justin is describing not the universal, but only the prevailing and prominent character of his teaching." ‡ And it is not a description of the teaching in the Fourth Gospel in particular, but a general statement, not inconsistent with the fact that the character of the discourses in the Fourth Gospel is in some respects peculiar. But, as to "brief and concise sayings" of Jesus, Professor Drummond, in glancing over the first thirteen chapters of John, finds no less than fifty-three to which this description would apply. He observes that "the book contains in reality very little connected argumentation; and even the longest discourses consist rather of successive pearls of thought strung on a thread of association than of consecutive discussion and proof." ‖ But it may be greatly doubted whether Justin means here by $\beta\rho\alpha\chi\epsilon\tilde{\iota}\varsigma\ \lambda\acute{o}\gamma o\iota$, as Tayler supposes, simply "short, aphoristic maxims." The reference to the Sophists, that is, rhetoricians, leads one rather to suppose that Justin is contrasting the $\lambda\acute{o}\gamma o\iota$, "discourses," of Christ in general with the long, artificial, argumentative, and rhetorical $\lambda\acute{o}\gamma o\iota$ of the Sophists among his earlier or later contemporaries, such as Dion Chrysostomus, Herodes Atticus, Polemo and Aristides, whom Philostratus describes in his biographies. As for brevity, the discourses in the Fourth Gospel are generally short: the longest continuous discourse there recorded

---

* *Sup. Rel.*, ii. 314; similarly J. J. Tayler, *An Attempt to ascertain the Character of the Fourth Gospel* (1867), p. 64; Davidson, *Introd. to the Study of the N.T.* (1868), ii. 386, and many others.

†*Apol.* i. 14: βραχεῖς δὲ καὶ σύντομοι παρ' αὐτοῦ λόγοι γεγόνασιν. It may be thought, perhaps, that οἱ has dropped out after σύντομοι, which might easily have happened. But, even if the article had been used, the argument would be worthless. Such general propositions are seldom to be taken without qualification.

‡ *Theol. Review*, July, 1877, xiv. 330.

‖ *Ibid.* pp. 330, 331.

would hardly occupy five minutes in the reading. The Sermon on the Mount as given by Matthew is much longer than any unbroken discourse in John. But what characterizes the teaching of Christ in the Gospels, as Justin intimates, is the divine authority and spiritual power with which he speaks; and this is not less striking in the Fourth Gospel than in the Synoptists. (Comp. Matt. vii. 29; Luke iv. 32; John vii. 26, 46.)

A more plausible objection is this. If Justin knew and used the Fourth Gospel at all, why has he not used it more? Why has he never appealed to it in proof of his doctrine of the Logos and of the pre-existence of Christ? He has expressly quoted but one saying of Christ recorded in it, and one of John the Baptist, and has referred to but one incident peculiar to it, unless we adopt the view of Professor Drummond respecting his reference to John xix. 13. (See above, p. 50.) His account of Christ's life and teaching corresponds substantially with that given in the Synoptic Gospels, which he follows (so it is affirmed) where they differ, or seem to differ, from John. Albrecht Thoma, in an article in Hilgenfeld's *Zeitschrift*, comes to the conclusion, after a minute examination of the subject, that Justin "knows and uses almost every chapter of the Logos-Gospel, and in part very fully." But such considerations as I have mentioned convince him, notwithstanding, that he did not regard it as apostolic, or historically authentic. He finds Justin's relation to the Apostle Paul very similar. Justin shows himself well acquainted with Paul's writings, he often follows him in his citations from the Old Testament where they differ from the Septuagint, he borrows largely his thoughts and illustrations and language, but never quotes him expressly and by name; and so Mr. Thoma thinks he cannot have regarded him as an Apostle.*

This argument forgets the nature of Justin's writings. Were he addressing a Christian community in defence of his

---

* See the article, "Justins literarisches Verhältniss zu Paulus und zum Johannes-Evangelium," in Hilgenfeld's *Zeitschrift für wissensch. Theologie*, 1875, xviii. 383 ff., 490 ff. The quotation in the text is from p. 553.

doctrine of the pre-existence and subordinate deity of Christ in opposition to the Ebionites, these objections would be valid. But he was writing for unbelievers. In his Apologies addressed to the Emperor and Senate and people of Rome, he cannot quote the Christian writings in *direct* proof of the truth of Christian doctrines, and makes no attempt to do so. In giving the account which he does of the teaching of Christ, he draws mainly from the Sermon on the Mount, and in his sketch of the Gospel history follows mainly the guidance of Matthew, though also using Luke, and in two or three instances Mark. That is exactly what was to be expected. Justin's chief argument is derived from the fulfilment of Old Testament prophecies, and in this he naturally follows the Gospel of Matthew, which is distinguished from the others by its reference to them. Where Matthew's citations differ from the Alexandrine version of the Old Testament, Justin often appears to borrow from Matthew rather than from the Septuagint.* The discourses of Christ as they are given in the Synoptic Gospels were obviously much better fitted for his purpose of presenting to heathens a general view of Christ's teaching than those in the Gospel of John. Similar remarks apply to the Dialogue with Trypho the Jew. Here Dr. Davidson thinks it strange that Justin should not have quoted the prologue of the Fourth Gospel, and such a passage as "Before Abraham was, I am," in proof of Christ's divinity and pre-existence.† But the Jew with whom Justin was arguing would not have accepted an assertion of John or a declaration of Christ as a proof of its truth. So in the case of Paul's writings. Paul was not so popular among the Jews that his name would recommend the arguments or illustrations which Justin borrows from him; still less could Justin quote his Epistles in proof of doctrine in a discussion with a Jew, or in a defence of Christianity addressed to heathens.

---

* See Semisch, *Die apost. Denkwürdigkeiten* u.s.w., pp. 110-120; examples are also given by Norton, *Genuineness*, etc., vol. i. Addit. Notes, pp. ccxx., ccxxii., cccxxxii. f.

† Davidson's *Introd. to the Study of the N. T.* (1868), ii. 385. Compare Volkmar, *Ueber Justin den Märtyrer* u.s.w. (Zürich, 1853), p. 20 f.; *Ursprung uns. Evang.* (1866), p. 107 f. Thoma, *ubi supra*, p. 556.

The correctness of this explanation is confirmed by an indisputable fact. Justin certainly believed that the Apostle John was the author of the Apocalypse; *Supernatural Religion* (i. 295) thinks that this was the only book of the New Testament which he regarded as "inspired"; Thoma (p. 563, note 1) even supposes that it was read in the churches in Justin's time together with the "Memoirs" and the Prophets of the Old Testament. How, then, does it happen that he has not a single quotation from this book, which calls Christ "the Word [Logos] of God" (Rev. xix. 13), "the beginning of the creation of God" (iii. 14), "the first and the last and the living one" (i. 17, comp. ii. 8), "the searcher of the reins and hearts" (ii. 23), and, apparently (though according to Alford and Westcott not really), "the Alpha and the Omega, the beginning and the end" (xxii. 13)? In speaking of the different opinions among Christians about the resurrection, Justin once refers to the book as agreeing with the prophets in predicting the Millennium, and mentions the name of the author (*Dial.* c. 81; the passage will be cited below); but, as I have said, he nowhere *quotes* this work, which he regarded as inspired, apostolic, prophetic, though it contains so much which might seem to favor his view of the person of Christ. Were it not for that almost accidental reference to it, it might be plausibly argued that he was ignorant of its existence. In one place in the Dialogue with Trypho (c. 18), Justin half apologizes for subjoining "some brief sayings" of the Saviour to the words of the Prophets, on the ground that Trypho had acknowledged that he had read the precepts of Christ "in the so-called Gospel" (*Dial.* c. 10). But he does not introduce them there as arguments.

It should be observed, further, that the course pursued by Justin in abstaining from quoting the Gospels in proof of doctrines, and in not mentioning the Evangelists by name, in writings addressed to unbelievers, is simply that which was followed, with slight exceptions, by a long line of Christian Apologists from his time down to that of Eusebius.*

---

* See Norton, *Gen. of the Gospels*, i. 218 ff.; Westcott, *Canon of the N.T.*, p. 116 ff.; E. S. Ffoulkes, art. *Fathers*, in Smith and Wace's *Dict. of Christian Biog.*, ii. 456 f.

It may still be said that this applies only to quotations made in proof of *doctrines*. It may be asked, and there is some force in the question, Why has not Justin used John as he has used the Synoptic Gospels, as an authority for historical facts, for facts which he supposed to be predicted in the Old Testament? To take one example which has been urged: Justin has quoted from the Old Testament, in precisely the same form as John (differing from the established text of the Septuagint), the words, "They shall look on me whom they pierced":* but instead of referring to the incident which led John to quote it, — the thrusting of a spear into our Saviour's side by a Roman soldier, — he seems to apply it to the crucifixion generally. How could he do this, if he accepted the Gospel of John? †

This case presents little difficulty. The verbs in the quotation, it will be observed, are in the plural. If Justin regarded the prophecy as including the act of the Roman soldier, he could not have restricted it to that: he must have regarded the language of the Old Testament as referring also to the piercing of the hands and the feet of Jesus on the part of the soldiers who nailed him to the cross. It is not strange, therefore, that he should quote the passage without referring to the particular act mentioned by John. He applies the prophecy, moreover, to the Jews, who *caused* the death of Jesus, and not to the Roman soldiers, who were the immediate agents in the crucifixion.‡

But there is a stronger case than this. Justin, who speaks of Christ as "the passover" or paschal lamb, symbolizing the deliverance of Christian believers from death, "as the blood of the passover saved those who were in Egypt" (*Dial.* c. 111, comp. 40), has not noticed the fact recorded by John alone, that the legs of Christ were not broken by the Roman soldiers at the crucifixion. This the Evangelist regards as a fulfilment of the scripture, "A bone of him shall not be

---

* Zech. xii. 10; John xix. 37; Justin, *Apol.* i. 52. See above, p. 46.

† Thoma, pp. 542 f., 556; comp. Engelhardt, *Das Christenthum Justins des Märtyrers* (1878), p. 350.

‡ *Apol.* i. 52; *Dial.* cc. 14, 32, 64, 118; comp. *Dial.* cc. 85, 93, etc.; Acts ii. 23; x. 39.

broken"; and this quotation is commonly referred to the direction respecting the paschal lamb (Ex. xii. 46; Num. ix. 12). How, it may be asked, could Justin, with his fondness for types, have neglected such a fulfilment as this, when the Evangelist had already pointed it out? This argument is plausible, and has some weight. Let us consider it.

In the first place, I must venture to doubt whether there is any reference in John to the paschal lamb at all. The Evangelist says nothing whatever to indicate such a reference, though some explanation would seem to be needed of the transformation of a precept into a prediction. The language of Ps. xxxiv. 20 (Sept. xxxiii. 21) corresponds more closely with the citation; and, considering the free way in which passages of the Old Testament are applied in the New, the fact that in the connection in which the words stand in the Psalm protection of life is referred to does not seem a very serious objection to the supposition that the Evangelist had this passage in mind. He may well have regarded the part of the Psalm which he quotes as fulfilled in the case of "Jesus Christ the righteous" in the incident which he records, and the preceding verse as fulfilled in the resurrection. And some eminent scholars take this view of his meaning; so, *e.g.*, Grotius, Wetstein, Bishop Kidder, Hammond, Whitby, Brückner, Bäumlein, Weiss;* others, as Lenfant and Le Clerc, leave the matter doubtful; and some, as Vitringa and Bengel, suppose the Evangelist to have had both passages in mind. But, waiving this question, I would say, once for all, that very little importance is to be attached to this sort of *a priori* reasoning. We may be surprised that Justin should not have been led by the Fourth Gospel to find here a fulfilment of prophecy of some sort, and to use it in his argument; but a hundred cases equally surprising might be cited of the neglect of a writer to use an argument or to recognize a fact which we should have confidently expected that he would use or recognize. To take the first that lies at hand. I have before me the work of Dr. Sanday,

---

* *Bibl. Theol. des N.T.*, 3e Aufl. (1880), p. 638; comp. his *Der Johanneische Lehrbegriff* (1862), p. 114, note. So R. H. Hutton, *Essays, Theol. and Literary*, 2d ed. (1880), i. 195.

The Gospels in the Second Century, a learned, elaborate, and valuable treatise in reply to *Supernatural Religion*. He adduces from all sources the evidence of the use of the Gospels by writers who flourished in the period from Clement of Rome to Clement of Alexandria and Tertullian, including those whose references to the Gospel are very slight and doubtful, or of whom mere fragments remain. Appended to the work is a chronological and analytical table of these authors. But, on looking it over, we find no mention of Theophilus, bishop of Antioch A.D. 169–181; and Dr. Sanday has nowhere presented the testimony of this writer, though we have from him an elaborate "Apology" or defence of Christianity in three books, in which he quotes several passages from the Gospel of Matthew with the introduction, "The evangelic voice teaches" so and so, or "the Gospel says,"* and though, as we have seen, he quotes the Gospel of John (ch. i. 1, 3), naming the Evangelist, and describing him as one moved by the Spirit of God (see above, p. 58). He is in fact the earliest writer who does thus expressly quote the Fourth Gospel as the work of John. Now suppose Dr. Sanday was a Father of the third or fourth century who had composed a treatise with the purpose of collecting the evidences of the use of the Gospels by early Christian writers. What would the author of *Supernatural Religion* say to the facts in this case? Would he not argue that Sandæus could not possibly have been acquainted with this work of Theophilus, and that the pretended "Apology" was probably spurious? And, if he found in Sandæus (p. 303) a single apparent allusion to that writer, would he not maintain that this must be an interpolation? — Or to take another example. Sandæus is examining the question about Justin Martyr's use of the Gospels, and observes that "he says emphatically that all the children ($\pi\acute{\alpha}\nu\tau\alpha\varsigma$ $\acute{\alpha}\pi\lambda\tilde{\omega}\varsigma$ $\tau o\grave{\upsilon}\varsigma$ $\pi\alpha\tilde{\iota}\delta\alpha\varsigma$) in Bethlehem were slain, without mentioning the limitation of age given in St. Matthew" (p. 106; comp. Justin, *Dial.* c. 78). Now in our present texts of Justin there is another

---

* *Ad Autol.* lib. iii. cc. 13, 14, ed. Otto; comp. Matt. v. 28, 44, 46; vi. 3.

reference to the slaughter of the innocents, in which Herod is represented as "destroying all the children born in Bethlehem *at that time*." * But here *Supernatural Religion* might argue, It is certain that this qualifying phrase could not have been in the copy used by Sandæus, who takes no notice of the passage, though his aim is to meet the objections to the genuineness of our Gospels. Is it not clear that the words were interpolated by some one who wished to bring Justin into harmony with Matthew? Would Justin be so inconsistent with himself as that addition would make him?

A multitude of questions may be asked, to which no particular answer can be given, in reference to the use which Justin and writers in all ages have made of our Gospels. We cannot say why he has quoted this saying of Jesus and not that, or referred to this incident in the history and not that; why, for example, in his account of Christ's teaching in his First Apology, he makes no allusion to any of the parables which form so remarkable a feature of it, and quotes from them in but one place in his Dialogue with Trypho (*Dial.* c. 125). We can only say that he had to stop somewhere; † that he has used the Gospels much more freely than any other of the many Christian Apologists whose writings have come down to us from his day to that of Lactantius and Eusebius; that his selection of the sayings of Christ seems on the whole judicious and natural, though many pearls of great price are missing; that the historical incidents by which he supports his special argument from the fulfilment of prophecy are for the most part what might be expected; and that it was natural that in general he should follow the Synoptic Gospels rather than that of John.‡ But one needs only to try experiments on particular works by almost any writer to find that great caution is required in drawing inferences from what he has *not* done.

**Dial.* c. 103: ἀνελόντος πάντας τοὺς ἐν Βηθλεὲμ ἐκείνου τοῦ καιροῦ γεννηθέντας παῖδας.

† Comp. *Apol.* i. 52: "Here we conclude, though we have many other prophecies to produce."

‡ See on this point Meyer, *Komm. über d. Ev. Joh.*, 5e Aufl. (1869), p. 8 f., note (Eng. trans., p. 8 f., note 3); comp. Weizsäcker, *Untersuchungen über d. evang. Geschichte*, p. 229.

As to the case before us, Justin may not have thought of the incident peculiar to the Fourth Gospel, or he may have considered, and very reasonably too, that an argument for the typical character of the paschal lamb founded on the direction given in the Pentateuch about the bones, or an argument *assuming* the Messianic reference of the passage in the Psalms, was not well adapted to convince unbelievers. Perhaps he had urged this argument in the actual dialogue with Trypho, and had encountered objections to its validity which he did not find it easy to answer. This may seem more probable than the supposition of forgetfulness. But will you say that such a failure of memory as has been suggested is incredible? Let us compare a case. One of the most distinguished scholars of this country, in an article published in the American Biblical Repository, remarks, in the course of an elaborate argument: —

> The particulars inserted or omitted by different Evangelists vary exceedingly from each other, some inserting what others omit, and some narrating at length what others briefly touch. *E. g.*, compare the history of the temptation by Mark, and even by Matthew and Luke; and where is the history of the *transfiguration* to be found, except in Matthew?*

Could anything be *a priori* more incredible than that an eminent Biblical scholar, who when this was written had held the office of Professor of Sacred Literature in the Andover Theological Seminary for nearly thirty years, should have forgotten that both Mark and Luke have given full accounts of the transfiguration, the latter especially mentioning a number of important particulars not found in Matthew? † If Professor Stuart was occasionally guilty of oversights, — as who is not? — he certainly had a clearer head and a better memory than Justin Martyr, who in quoting and referring to the Old Testament makes not a few extraordinary mistakes.‡

I admit that some weight should be allowed to the argu-

---

* *American Biblical Repository*, October, 1838, xii. 341.

† Compare Mark ix. 2-8 and Luke ix. 28-36 with Matt. xvii. 1-8.

‡ See the references already given, p. 49, note*; also *Some Account of the Writings and Opinions of Justin Martyr*, by John [Kaye], Bishop of Lincoln, 3d ed. (1853), pp. 139 f. 148; comp. p. 129 f.

ment we have been examining, so far as reference to the history in the Gospel of John is concerned; but it does not seem to me that much importance should be attached to it. The tradition in the Synoptic Gospels represents without doubt the substance of the apostolic preaching; it was earlier committed to writing than that contained in the Fourth Gospel; the incidents of the threefold narrative were more familiar; and the discourses, especially, as has already been remarked, were far better fitted for illustrating the general character of Christ's teaching than those of the Fourth Gospel. It would have been very strange, therefore, if in such works as those of Justin the Synoptic Gospels had not been mainly used.

Engelhardt, the most recent writer on Justin, is impressed by the facts which Thoma presents respecting Justin's relation to John, but comes to a different conclusion. He thinks Justin could never have made the use of John's Gospel which he has done, if he had not regarded it as genuine. It purports to be a work of the beloved disciple. The conjecture that by "the disciple whom Jesus loved" Andrew was intended (Lützelberger), or Nathanael (Spaeth), or a personified ideal conception (Scholten), was reserved for the sagacity of critics of the nineteenth century: there is no trace that in Christian antiquity this title ever suggested any one but John. The Gospel must have been received as his work, or rejected as fictitious. Engelhardt believes that Justin received it, and included it in his "Memoirs"; but he conjectures that with it there was commonly read in the churches and used by Justin a Harmony of the first three Gospels, or at least of Matthew and Luke, while the Fourth Gospel, not yet incorporated into the Harmony, stood in the background.* I do not feel the need of this hypothesis; but it may deserve consideration.

It is objected further that Justin's statements repeatedly contradict the Fourth Gospel, and that he cannot therefore have regarded it as apostolic or authentic. For example, he follows the Synoptic Gospels, so Hilgenfeld and David-

---

* See Engelhardt, *Das Christenthum Justins des Märtyrers*, pp. 345-352.

son and *Supernatural Religion* affirm, in placing, in opposition to John, the death of Christ on the 15th of Nisan, the day after the paschal lamb was killed.

The argument that Justin cannot have accepted the Gospel of John because he has followed the Synoptists in respect to the day of Christ's death hardly needs an answer. If the discrepancy referred to, whether real or not, did not prevent the whole Christian world from accepting John and the Synoptic Gospels alike in the last quarter of the second century, it need not have hindered Justin from doing so at an earlier date. But it is far from certain that Hilgenfeld and Davidson have correctly interpreted the language of Justin: "It is written that you seized him on the day of the passover, and in like manner crucified him at [*or* during] the passover (ἐν τῷ πάσχα)."* Meyer understands this as placing the death of Jesus on the day of the passover;† Otto in an elaborate note on the passage in his *third* edition of Justin's Works maintains the same view;‡ Thoma regards the language as ambiguous.‖ I will not undertake to pronounce an opinion upon so difficult a question, as the objection is futile on any supposition.

Again, *Supernatural Religion* asserts that "Justin contradicts the Fourth Gospel, in limiting the work of Jesus to one year." (*S. R.* ii. 313.) Dr. Davidson makes the same statement;** but neither he nor *S. R.* adduces any proof of it. I know of no passage in Justin which affirms or implies this limitation. But, if such a passage should be found, the argument against Justin's reception of the Fourth Gospel would

---

* Dial. c. 111. See Hilgenfeld, *Der Paschastreit der alten Kirche* (1860), pp. 205-209; Davidson, *Introd. to the Study of the N.T.* (1868), ii. 384; *Sup. Rel.*, ii. 313; comp. Wieseler, *Beiträge* (1869), p. 240. — Note here the use of γέγραπται.

† *Komment. üb. d. Ev. des Joh.*, 5e Aufl. p. 24 f. (Eng. trans. i. 24 f.) Steitz, who formerly agreed with Hilgenfeld, afterwards adopted the view of Meyer; see the art. *Pascha* in Herzog's *Real-Encyk. f. Prot. u. Kirche*, xi. 151, note *.

‡ *Ivstini . . . Martyris Opera*, tom. i. pars ii., ed. tert. (1877), p. 395 f. Otto cites *Dial.* c. 99, where the agony in Gethsemane is referred to as taking place "on the day on which Jesus was to be crucified," as showing that Justin followed the Jewish reckoning of the day from sunset to sunset. Davidson takes no notice of this. If Meyer and Otto are right, we have here a strong argument for Justin's use of the Fourth Gospel.

‖ *Ubi supra*, p. 535 f.

** *Introd. to the Study of the N.T.*, ii. 387.

be worthless. The opinion that Christ's ministry lasted but one year, or little more, was held by many in the early Church who received the Gospel of John without question. It was maintained by the Basilidians, the Valentinians, and the author of the Clementine Homilies, by Clement of Alexandria, Tertullian, Origen, Julius Africanus, Pseudo-Cyprian, Archelaus, Lactantius, Ephraem Syrus apparently, Philastrius, Gaudentius, Q. Julius Hilarianus, Augustine apparently, Evagrius the presbyter, and others among the Fathers, and has been held by modern scholars, as Bentley, Mann, Priestley (*Harmony*), Lant Carpenter (*Harmony*), and Henry Browne (*Ordo Sæclorum*).* The Fathers were much influenced by their interpretation of Isa. lxi. 2, — " to preach the acceptable year of the Lord," — quoted in Luke iv. 19. It is true that John vi. 4 is against this view; but its defenders find means, satisfactory to themselves, of getting over the difficulty.

Other objections urged by Dr. Davidson and *Supernatural Religion* seem to me too weak to need an answer. I will, however, notice one which is brought forward with great confidence by Thoma, who says "Justin directly contradicts the Fourth Gospel" (p. 556), and after him by F. C. J. van Goens, who introduces it with the words *enfin et surtout*.†

---

*The Basilidians, see Clem. Alex. *Strom*. i. 21, p. 408.—Valentinians, see Iren. *Hær*. i. 3. (al. 5), § 3; ii. 20. (al. 36), § 1; 22. (al. 38–40), §§ 1–6.—Clem. Hom. xvii. 19.—Clem. Alex. *Strom*. i. 21, p. 407; vi. 11, p. 783, l. 40; comp. v. 6, p. 668; vii. 17, p. 898.—Tertull. *Adv. Jud*. c. 8; *Marc*. i. 15 (but here are different readings).—Origen, *De Princip*. iv. 5, Opp. i. 160; *In Levit. Hom*. ix. c. 5, Opp. ii. 239; *In Luc. Hom*. xxxii., Opp. iii. 970; contra, *In Matt. Comm. Ser*., c. 40, Opp. iii. 859, "fere tres annos"; comp. *Cels*. ii. 12, Opp. i. 397, οὐδὲ τρία ἔτη.—Jul. Africani *Chron*. frag. l. ap. Routh, *Rell. Sacræ*, ii. 301 f., ed. alt.—Pseudo-Cyprian, *De Paschæ Comp*. (A.D. 243), c. 22.—Archelai et Manetis Disp., c. 34.—Lactant. *Inst*. iv. 10. (*De Morte Persec*. c. 2.)—Ephraem, *Serm*. xiii. *in Nat. Dom*., Opp. Syr. ii. 432.—Philastr. *Hær*. 106.—Gaudent. *Serm*. iii., Migne, *Patrol. Lat*. xx. 865.—Hilarianus, *De Mundi Dur*. (A.D. 397) c. 16; *De Die Paschæ*, c. 15; Migne, xiii. 1104, 1114, or Gallandi, *Bibl. Patr*. viii. 238, 748.—Augustine, *De Civ. Dei*, xviii. 54, Opp. vii. 866; *Ad Hesych. Epist*. 199 (al. 80), § 20, Opp. ii. 1122; contra, *De Doct. Christ*. ii. 42 (al. 28), Opp. iii. 66.—Evagrius presbyter(*cir*. A.D. 423), *Alterc. inter Theoph. Christ. et Sim. Jud*., Migne xx. 1176, or Gallandi, ix. 254.—So also the author of the treatise *De Promissis et Prædictionibus Dei* (published with the works of Prosper Aquitanus), pars i. c. 7; pars v. c. 2; Migne, li. 739 c, 855 b.—Browne, *Ordo Sæclorum* (Corrections and Additions), also cites Cyril of Alexandria, *In Isa*. xxxii. 10, Opp. ii. 446 d e, but this rests on a false inference; see, *contra*, Cyril, *In Isa*. xxix. 1, Opp. ii. 408 b. Besides the works of Nicholas Mann, *De veris Annis Jesu Christi natali et emortuali*, Lond. 1752, p. 158 ff., Greswell, *Dissertations*, etc., i. 438 ff., 2d ed. (1837), and Henry Browne, *Ordo Sæclorum*, Lond. 1844, p. 80 ff., one may consult especially F. X. Patritius (*i.e*. Patrizi), *De Evangeliis* (Friburg. Brisgov. 1853), lib. iii., diss. xix., p. 171 ff.

† *Revue de théologie et de philosophie*, Lausanne, 1878, xi. 92 f.

Justin speaks of Christ as "keeping silence and refusing any longer to make any answer to any one before Pilate, as has been declared in the Memoirs by the Apostles" (*Dial.* c. 102). M. van Goens remarks, "No one who had ever read the Fourth Gospel could speak in this way." What does M. van Goens think of Tertullian, who says,* "Velut agnus coram tondente se sine voce, sic non aperuit os suum. Hic enim *Pilato interrogante nihil locutus est*"? If Justin had even said that Christ made no answer when Pilate questioned him, this would be sufficiently explained by John xix. 9, to which Tertullian perhaps refers. But the expressions "no longer" and "*before* Pilate" lead rather to the supposition that Justin refers to Matt. xxvii. 11–14 and Mark xv. 2–5 (οὐκέτι οὐδὲν ἀπεκρίθη, "he no longer made any answer"), which certainly there is nothing in John to contradict.

Finally, the author of *Supernatural Religion* urges, generally, that in citing the Old Testament Justin, according to Semisch's count, refers to the author by name or by book one hundred and ninety-seven times, and omits to do this only one hundred and seventeen times. On the other hand, in referring to the words of Christ or the facts of Christian history for which he relied on the "Memoirs," he never cites the book (*S. R.* regards the "Memoirs" as one book) by the name of the author, except in a single instance, where he refers to "Peter's Memoirs" (*Dial.* c. 106).† "The inference," he says, "must not only be that he attached small importance to the Memoirs, but was actually ignorant of the author's name" (*S. R.* i. 297). That Justin attached small importance to the "Memoirs by the Apostles" on which he professedly relied for the teaching and life of Christ, and this, as *S. R.* contends, to the exclusion of oral tradition (*S. R.* i. 298), is an "inference" and a proposition which would surprise us in almost any other writer. The inference, moreover, that Justin "was actually ignorant of the author's name," when in one instance, according to *S. R.*,

---

* *Adv. Jud.* c. 13, Opp. ii. 737, ed. Œhler.
† See above, p. 20 f.

"he indicates Peter" as the author (*S. R.* i. 285), and when, as *S. R.* maintains, "the Gospel according to Peter," or "the Gospel according to the Hebrews" (which he represents as substantially the same work), was in all probability the source from which the numerous quotations in his works differing from our Gospels are taken,* is another specimen of singular logic. So much for generalities. But a particular objection to the conclusion that the Gospel of John was one of Justin's "Memoirs" is founded on the fact that he has never quoted or referred to it under the name of the author, though he has named the Apostle John as the author of the Apocalypse. (*S. R.* i. 298.) Great stress is laid on this contrast by many writers.

Let us see to what these objections amount. In the first place, the *way* in which Justin has mentioned John as the author of the Apocalypse is in itself enough to explain why he should not have named him in citing the "Memoirs." In his Dialogue with Trypho, after having quoted prophecies of the Old Testament in proof of his doctrine of the Millennium, — a doctrine in which he confesses some Christians did not agree with him, — he wishes to state that his belief is supported by a Christian writing which he regards as inspired and prophetic. He accordingly refers to the work as follows: "And afterwards also a certain man among us, whose name was John, one of the Apostles of Christ, in a revelation made by him prophesied that the believers in our Christ should spend a thousand years in Jerusalem," etc. (*Dial.* c. 81.) The Apostle John was certainly as well known outside of the Christian body as any other of the Evangelists; but we see that he is here introduced to Trypho as a stranger. Still more would he and the other Evangelists be strangers to the Roman Emperor and Senate, to whom the Apologies were addressed. That Justin under such circumstances should quote the Evangelists by name, assigning this saying or incident to "the Gospel according to Matthew," that to "Luke," and the other to "the Gospel according to John,"

---

* *Supernatural Religion*, i. 321; comp. pp. 312, 323, 332, 398, 416, 418–427; ii. 311, 7th ed.

as if he were addressing a Christian community familiar with the books, would have been preposterous. Justin has *described* the books in his First Apology as Memoirs of Christ, resting on the authority of the Apostles, and received by the Christians of his time as authentic records. That was all that his purpose required: the names of four unknown persons would have added no weight to his citations. In the Dialogue, he is even more specific in his description of the "Memoirs" than in the Apology. But to suppose that he would quote them as he quotes the books of the Old Testament with which Trypho was familiar is to ignore all the proprieties and congruities of the case.

This view is confirmed and the whole argument of *Supernatural Religion* is nullified by the fact that the general practice of Christian Apologists down to the time of Eusebius corresponds with that of Justin, as we have before had occasion to remark. (See above, p. 65.) It may be added that, while in writings addressed to Christian readers by the earlier Fathers the Old Testament is often, or usually, cited with reference to the author or book, the cases are comparatively very rare in which the Evangelists are named. For example, Clement of Alexandria, according to Semisch, quotes the Old Testament writers or books far oftener than otherwise by name, while in his very numerous citations from the Gospels he names John but three times, Matthew twice, Luke twice, and Mark once; in the countless citations of the Gospels in the Apostolical Constitutions, the Evangelists are never named; and so in the numerous quotations of the Gospels in Cyprian's writings, with the exception of a single treatise (the *Testimonia* or *Ad Quirinum*), the names of the Evangelists are never mentioned. But it cannot be necessary to expose further the utter futility of this objection, which has so often been inconsiderately urged.*

In this view of the objections to the supposition that Justin used the Gospel of John and included it in his

---

*See Semisch, *Die apostol. Denkwürdigkeiten*, u. s. w., p. 84 ff.; and compare Norton, *Genuineness*, etc., i. 205 ff., 2d ed.

"Memoirs," I have either cited them in the precise language of their authors, or have endeavored to state them in their most plausible form. When fairly examined, only one of them appears to have weight, and that not much. I refer to the objection that, if Justin used the Fourth Gospel at all, we should expect him to have used it more. It seems to me, therefore, that there is nothing of importance to countervail the very strong presumption from different lines of evidence that the "Memoirs" of Justin Martyr, "composed by Apostles and their companions," were our four Gospels.

A word should perhaps be added in reference to the view of Dr. E. A. Abbott, in the valuable article *Gospels* contributed to the new edition of the Encyclopædia Britannica. He holds that Justin's "Memoirs" included the first three Gospels, and these only. These alone were received by the Christian community of his time as the authentic records of the life and teaching of Christ. If so, how can we explain the fact that a pretended Gospel so different in character from these, and so inconsistent with them as it is supposed to be, should have found universal acceptance in the next generation on the part of Christians of the most opposite opinions, without trace of controversy, with the slight exception of the Alogi previously mentioned ? *

I have not attempted in the present paper a thorough discussion of Justin Martyr's quotations, but only to illustrate by some decisive examples the false assumptions on which the reasoning of *Supernatural Religion* is founded. In a full treatment of the subject, it would be necessary to consider the question of Justin's use of apocryphal Gospels, and in particular the "Gospel according to the Hebrews" and the "Gospel according to Peter," which figure so prominently in what calls itself "criticism" (*die Kritik*) as the pretended source of Justin's quotations. This subject has already been

---

* See above, p. 18. The work of Hippolytus, of which we know only the title found on the cathedra of his statue at Rome, "On [*or* "In defence of" ($\hat{v}\pi\grave{\epsilon}\rho$)] the Gospel according to John and the Apocalypse," may have been written in answer to their objections. See Bunsen's *Hippolytus*, 2d ed. (1854), i. 460. On the Alogi see also Weizsäcker, *Untersuchungen über d. evang. Geschichte*, p. 226 f., note.

referred to;* but it is impossible to treat it here in detail. In respect to "the Gospel according to the Hebrews" I will give in a Note some quotations from the article *Gospels, Apocryphal*, by Professor R. A. Lipsius, of Jena, in the second volume of Smith and Wace's *Dictionary of Christian Biography*, published in the present year, with extracts from other recent writers, which will sufficiently show how groundless is the supposition that Justin's quotations were mainly derived from this Gospel.† Lipsius certainly will not be suspected of any "apologetic" tendency. Credner's hypothesis that the "Gospel according to Peter," which he regards as the Gospel used by the Jewish Christians generally, and strangely identifies with the *Diatessaron* of Tatian, was the chief source of Justin's quotations, was thoroughly refuted by Mr. Norton as long ago as the year 1834 in the *Select Journal of Foreign Periodical Literature*, and afterwards in a Note to the first edition of his work on the Genuineness of the Gospels.‡ It is exposed on every side to overwhelming objections, and has hardly a shadow of evidence to support it. Almost our whole knowledge of this Gospel is derived from the account of it by Serapion, bishop of Antioch near the end of the second century (A.D. 191–213), who is the first writer by whom it is mentioned.∥ He "found it for the most part in accordance with the right doctrine of the Saviour," but containing passages favoring the opinions of the Docetæ, by whom it was used. According to Origen, it represented the "brethren" of Jesus as sons of Joseph by a former wife.** It was evidently a book of very little note. Though it plays a conspicuous part in the speculations of modern German scholars and of *Supernatural Religion* about

---

*See above, p. 15 f.

† See Note C, at the end of this essay.

‡ *Select Journal*, etc. (Boston), April, 1834, vol. iii., part ii., pp. 234-242; *Evidences of the Genuineness of the Gospels*, vol. i. (1837), Addit. Notes, pp. ccxxxii.-cclv. See also Bindemann, who discusses ably the whole question about Justin Martyr's Gospels, in the *Theol. Studien u. Kritiken*, 1842, pp. 355-482; Semisch, *Die apostol. Denkwürdigkeiten* u. s. w., pp. 43-59; on the other side, Credner, *Beiträge* u. s. w., vol. i. (1832); Mayerhoff, *Hist.-crit. Einleitung in die petrinischen Schriften* (1835), p. 234 ff.; Hilgenfeld, *Krit. Untersuchungen* u. s. w., p. 259 ff.

∥ Serapion's account of it is preserved by Eusebius, *Hist. Eccl.* vi. 12.

**Origen, *Comm. in Matt.* t. x. § 17, Opp. iii. 462 f.

the origin of the Gospels and the quotations of Justin Martyr, *not a single fragment of it has come down to us.* This *nominis umbra* has therefore proved wonderfully convenient for those who have had occasion, in support of their hypotheses, "to draw unlimited cheques," as Lightfoot somewhere expresses it, "on the bank of the unknown." Mr. Norton has shown, by an acute analysis of Serapion's account of it, that in all probability it was not an historical, but a doctrinal work.* Lipsius remarks: "The statement of Theodoret (*Hær. Fab.* ii. 2) that the Nazarenes had made use of this Gospel rested probably on a misunderstanding. The passage moreover in Justin Martyr (*Dial. c. Tryph.* 106) in which some have thought to find mention of the *Memorials of Peter* is very doubtful. . . . Herewith fall to the ground all those hypotheses which make the *Gospel of Peter* into an original work made use of by Justin Martyr, nigh related to the *Gospel of the Hebrews,* and either the Jewish Christian basis of our canonical St. Mark [so Hilgenfeld], or, at any rate, the Gospel of the Gnosticizing Ebionites" [Volkmar]. † To this I would only add that almost the only fact of which we are directly informed respecting the contents of the so-called "Gospel of Peter" is that it favored the opinions of the Docetæ, to which Justin Martyr, who wrote a book against the Marcionites (Euseb. *Hist. Eccl.* iv. 11. § 8), was diametrically opposed.

Glancing back now over the ground we have traversed, we find (1) that the general reception of our four Gospels as sacred books throughout the Christian world in the time of Irenæus makes it almost certain that the "Memoirs called Gospels," "composed by Apostles and their companions," which were used by his early contemporary Justin Martyr, and were read in the Christian churches of his day as the authoritative records of Christ's life and teaching, were the same books; (2) that this presumption is confirmed by the actual use which Justin has made of all our Gospels, though

---

* *Genuineness of the Gospels,* 2d ed., vol. iii. (1848), pp. 255-260; abridged edition (1867), pp. 362-366.

† Smith and Wace's *Dict. of Christian Biog.*, ii. 712.

he has mainly followed, as was natural, the Gospel of Matthew, and his *direct* citations from the Gospel of John, and references to it, are few; (3) that it is still further strengthened, in respect to the Gospel of John, by the evidences of its use between the time of Justin and that of Irenæus, both by the Catholic Christians and the Gnostics, and especially by its inclusion in Tatian's *Diatessaron;* (4) that, of the two principal assumptions on which the counter-argument is founded, one is demonstrably false and the other baseless ; and (5) that the particular objections to the view that Justin included the Gospel of John in his "Memoirs" are of very little weight. We are authorized then, I believe, to regard it as in the highest degree probable, if not morally certain, that in the time of Justin Martyr the Fourth Gospel was generally received as the work of the Apostle John.

WE pass now to our third point, the use of the Fourth Gospel by the various Gnostic sects. The length to which the preceding discussion has extended makes it necessary to treat this part of the subject in a very summary manner.

The Gnostic sects with which we are concerned became conspicuous in the second quarter of the second century, under the reigns of Hadrian (A.D. 117–138) and Antoninus Pius (A.D. 138–161). The most prominent among them were those founded by Marcion, Valentinus, and Basilides. To these may be added the Ophites or Naassenes.

Marcion has already been referred to.* He prepared a Gospel for his followers by striking from the Gospel of Luke what was inconsistent with his system, and treated in a similar manner ten of the Epistles of Paul. He rejected the other Gospels, not on the ground that they were spurious, but because he believed their authors were under the influence of Jewish prejudices.† In proof of this, he appealed to the passage in the Epistle to the Galatians on which Baur

---

* See above, p. 19.
† See Irenæus, *Hær*. iii. 12. § 12.

and his school lay so much stress. "Marcion," says Tertullian, "having got the Epistle of Paul to the Galatians, who reproves even the Apostles themselves for not walking straight, according to the truth of the Gospel, . . . endeavors to destroy the reputation of those Gospels which are truly such, and are published under the name of Apostles, or also of apostolic men, in order that he may give to his own the credit which he takes away from them." * In another place, Tertullian says, addressing Marcion: "If you had not rejected some and corrupted others of the Scriptures which contradict your opinion, the Gospel of John would have confuted you." † Again: "Of those historians whom we possess, it appears that Marcion *selected* Luke for his mutilations." ‡ The fact that Marcion placed his rejection of the Gospels on this ground, that the Apostles were but imperfectly enlightened, shows that he could not question their apostolic authorship. His reference to the Epistle to the Galatians indicates also that the "pillar-apostles" (Gal. ii. 9), Peter and John, were particularly in his mind. Peter, it will be remembered, was regarded as having sanctioned the Gospel of Mark. (See above, p. 21.)

It has been asserted by many modern critics, as Hilgenfeld, Volkmar, Scholten, Davidson, and others, that, if Marcion had been acquainted with the Gospel of John, he would have chosen that, rather than Luke, for expurgation, on account of its marked anti-Judaic character. But a careful comparison of John's Gospel with Marcion's doctrines will show that it contradicts them in so many places and so

---

* *Adv. Marc.* iv. 3. Comp. *Præscr*. cc. 22-24. See also Norton, *Genuineness of the Gospels*, 2d ed., iii. 206 ff., 303 ff.; or abridged edition, pp. 332 ff., 392 ff.

† *De Carne Christi*, c. 3.

‡ *Adv. Marc.* iv. 2. "Lucam videtur Marcion elegisse quem cæderet." On account of the use of *videtur* here, Dr. Davidson, following some German critics, says, "Even in speaking about Marcion's treatment of Luke, Tertullian puts it forth as a conjecture." (*Introd. to the Study of the N. T.*, ii. 305.) A *conjecture*, when Tertullian has devoted a whole book to the refutation of Marcion from those passages of Luke which he retained! The context and all the facts of the case show that no doubt can possibly have been intended; and Tertullian often uses *videri*, not in the sense of "to seem," but of "to be seen," "to be apparent." See *Apol.* c. 19; *De Orat.* c. 21; *Adv. Prax.* cc. 26, 29; *Adv. Jud.* c. 5, from Isa. i. 12; and *De Præscr.* c. 38, which has likewise been misinterpreted.

absolutely that it would have been utterly unsuitable for his purpose.*

The theosophic or speculative Gnostics, as the Ophites, Valentinians, and Basilidians, found more in John which, by ingenious interpretation, they could use in support of their systems.†

It is moreover to be observed, in regard to the Marcionites, as Mr. Norton remarks, "that their having recourse to the mutilation of Luke's Gospel shows that no other history of Christ's ministry existed more favorable to their doctrines; that, in the first half of the second century, when Marcion lived, there was no Gnostic Gospel in being to which he could appeal." ‡

We come now to Valentinus. It has already appeared that the later Valentinians, represented by Ptolemy, Heracleon, and the *Excerpta Theodoti*, received the Gospel of John without question. ‖ The presumption is therefore obviously very strong that it was so received by the founder of the sect. ** That this was so is the representation of Tertullian. He contrasts the course pursued by Marcion and Valentinus. "One man," he says, "perverts the Scriptures with his hand, another by his exposition of their meaning. For, if it appears that Valentinus uses the entire document,— *si Valentinus integro instrumento uti videtur*,— he has yet done violence to the truth more artfully than Marcion." For Marcion, he goes on to say, openly used the knife, not the pen; Valentinus has spared the Scriptures, but explains them away, or thrusts false meanings into them.††

---

*See on this point Bleek, *Einl. in d. N. T.*, 3d ed. (1875), p. 158, ff., with Mangold's note, who remarks that "it was simply impossible for Marcion to choose the fourth Gospel" for this purpose; also Weizsäcker, *Untersuchungen über d. evang. Geschichte* (1864), p. 230, ff.; Luthardt, *Die johan. Ursprung des vierten Ev.* (1874), p. 92, or Eng. trans., p. 108 f.; Godet, *Comm. sur l'évangile de St. Jean*, 2d ed., tom. i. (1876), p. 270 f., or Eng. trans., i. 222 f.

† On the use of the N.T. by the Valentinians, see particularly G. Heinrici, *Die valentinianische Gnosis und die Heilige Schrift*, Berlin, 1871.

‡ *Genuineness of the Gospels*, 2d ed., iii. 304; abridged ed., p. 392 f.

‖ See above, p. 60 f.

** On this point, see Norton, *Genuineness*, etc., 2d ed., iii. 321 f.; abridged ed., p. 403 f.

†† Tertullian, *Præscr.* c. 38. On the use of the word *videtur*, see above, p. 81, note ‡. The context shows that no doubt is intended. If, however, the word should be taken in the sense

The testimony of Tertullian is apparently confirmed by Hippolytus, who, in a professed account of the doctrines of Valentinus (*Ref. Hær.* vi. 21-37, or 16-32, Eng. trans.; comp. the introduction, § 3), says: "All the prophets, therefore, and the Law spoke from the Demiurgus, a foolish God, he says, [and spoke] as fools, knowing nothing. Therefore, says he, the Saviour says, 'All who have come before me are thieves and robbers' (John x. 8); and the Apostle, 'The mystery which was not made known to former generations'" (Eph. iii. 4, 5). Here, however, it is urged that Hippolytus, in his account of Valentinus, mixes up references to Valentinus and his followers in such a manner that we cannot be sure that, in the use of the φησί, "he says," he is not quoting from some one of his school, and not the master. A full exhibition of the facts and discussion of the question cannot be given here. I believe there is a strong presumption that Hippolytus *is* quoting from a work of Valentinus: the regular exposition of the opinions of his disciples, Secundus, Ptolemy, and Heracleon, does not begin till afterwards, in c. 38, or c. 33 of the English translation; but it is true that, in the present text, φησί is used vaguely toward the end of c. 35, where the opinions of the Italian and Oriental schools are distinguished in reference to a certain point. I therefore do not press this quotation as *direct* proof of the use of the Fourth Gospel by Valentinus himself.

Next to Marcion and Valentinus, the most eminent among the founders of early Gnostic sects was Basilides, of Alexandria. He flourished about A.D. 125. In the Homilies on Luke generally ascribed to Origen, though some have questioned their genuineness, we are told, in an account of apocryphal Gospels, that "Basilides had the audacity to write a Gospel according to Basilides."* Ambrose and Jerome copy this account in the prefaces to their re-

---

of "seems," the contrast must be between the ostensible use of the Scriptures by Valentinus and his virtual rejection of them by imposing upon them a sense contrary to their teaching. Comp. Irenæus, *Hær.* iii. 12. § 12: "scripturas quidem confitentes, interpretationes vero convertunt." So *Hær.* i. 3. § 6; iii. 14. § 4.

* So the Greek: Origen, *Hom.* i. *in Luc.*, Opp. iii. 932, note; the Latin in Jerome's translation reads, "Ausus fuit et Basilides scribere evangelium, et suo illud nomine titulare."

spective commentaries on Luke and Matthew; but there is no other notice of such a Gospel, or evidence of its existence, in all Christian antiquity, so far as is known. The work referred to could not have been a history of Christ's ministry, set up by Basilides and his followers in opposition to the Gospels received by the catholic Christians. In that case, we should certainly have heard of it from those who wrote in opposition to his heresy; but he and his followers are, on the contrary, represented as appealing to our Gospels of Matthew, Luke, and John;* and Hippolytus states expressly that the Basilidian account of all things concerning the Saviour subsequent to the birth of Jesus agreed with that given "in the Gospels." † The origin of the error is easily explained: a work in which Basilides set forth his view of the Gospel, *i.e.* of the teaching of Christ, might naturally be spoken of as "the Gospel according to Basilides." ‡ We have an account of such a work. Agrippa Castor, a contemporary of Basilides, and who, according to Eusebius, wrote a very able refutation of him, tells us that Basilides "composed twenty-four books on the Gospel," $\epsilon\iota\varsigma\ \tau\grave{o}$ $\epsilon\grave{\upsilon}\alpha\gamma\gamma\acute{\epsilon}\lambda\iota o\nu.$ ‖ Clement of Alexandria, who is one of our principal authorities for his opinions, cites his Ἐξηγητικά, "Expositions," or "Interpretations," quoting a long passage from "the twenty-third book." ** In the "Dispute between Archelaus and Manes," the "thirteenth treatise" of Basilides is cited, containing an explanation of the parable of the Rich Man and Lazarus.†† I agree with Dr. Hort in thinking it exceedingly probable that the work of Basilides which Hippolytus cites so often in his account of his opinions is the same which is quoted by Clement and Archelaus, and mentioned by Agrippa Castor.‡‡ Lipsius remarks:—

---

* Besides the work of Hippolytus, to be further noticed, see the passages from Clement of Alexandria and Epiphanius in Kirchhofer's *Quellensammlung*, p. 415 f.

† *Ref. Hær.* c. 27, or c. 16, Eng. trans.

‡ On this use of the term "Gospel," see Norton, *Genuineness*, etc., iii. 224 ff., or abridged edition, p. 343 f.

‖ Euseb. *Hist. Eccl.* iv. 7. §§ 6, 7.

** *Strom.* iv. 12, p. 599 f.

†† *Archelai et Manetis Disputatio*, c. 55, in Routh, *Rell. sacræ*, ed. alt., v. 197.

‡‡ See the art. *Basilides* in Smith and Wace's *Dict. of Christian Biog.*, vol. i. (1877), p. 271.

In any case, the work must have been an exposition of some Gospel by whose authority Basilides endeavored to establish his Gnostic doctrine. And it is anyhow most unlikely that he would have written a commentary on a Gospel of his own composition. Of our canonical Gospels, those of Matthew, Luke, and John, were used in his school; and from the fragments just referred to we may reasonably conclude that it was the Gospel of Luke on which he wrote his commentary.*

On this it may be observed, that the phrase of Agrippa Castor, "twenty-four books on *the* Gospel," excludes the idea that any particular Gospel, like that of Luke, could be intended. Such a Gospel would have been named or otherwise defined. The expression τὸ εὐαγγέλιον, if it refers to any book, must signify, in accordance with that use of the term which has before been illustrated,† "the Gospels" collectively. It is so understood by Norton,‡ Tischendorf, Luthardt, Godet, and others. It would not in itself *necessarily* denote precisely our *four* Gospels, though their use by Justin Martyr, and the fact that Luke and John are commented on by Basilides, and Matthew apparently referred to by him, would make it probable that they were meant.

There is, however, another sense of the word "Gospel" as used by Basilides,— namely, "the knowledge (*gnosis*) of supermundane things" (Hippol. *Ref. Hær.* vii. 27); and "the Gospel" in this sense plays a prominent part in his system as set forth by Hippolytus. The "twenty-four books on the Gospel" mentioned by Agrippa Castor, the "Expositions" or "Interpretations" of Clement, may perhaps have related to "the Gospel" in this sense. We cannot therefore, I think, argue confidently from this title that Basilides wrote a Commentary on our Four Gospels, though it naturally suggests this. It is evident, at any rate, that he supported his *gnosis* by far-fetched interpretations of the sayings of Christ as recorded in our Gospels; and that the supposition that he had a Gospel of his own composition, in the sense of a history of Christ's life and teaching, has not only no positive support of any strength, but is on various

---

* See the art. *Gospels* in the work just cited, ii. 715.
† See above, p. 22.
‡ See Norton's *Genuineness of the Gospels*, 2d ed., iii. 235-239, or abridged edition, p. 351 ff.

accounts utterly improbable. That he used an apocryphal Gospel *not* of his own composition is a supposition for which there is not a particle of evidence of any kind whatever.

I have spoken of Basilides as quoting the Gospel of John in the citations from him by Hippolytus. The passages are the following: "And this, he says, is what is said in the Gospels: 'The true light, which enlighteneth every man, was coming into the world.'" (*Ref. Hær.* vii. 22, or c. 10, Eng. trans.) The words quoted agree exactly with John i. 9 in the Greek, though I have adopted a different construction from that of the common version in translating. Again, "And that each thing, he says, has its own seasons, the Saviour is a sufficient witness, when he says, 'My hour is not yet come.'" (*Ref. Hær.* vii. 27, al. 15; John ii. 4.)

Here two objections are raised: first, that we cannot infer from the φησί, "he says," that Hippolytus is quoting from a treatise by Basilides himself; and, secondly, that the system of Basilides as set forth by Hippolytus represents a later development of the original scheme,—in other words, that he is quoting the writings and describing the opinions of the disciples of the school, and not of its founder.

To analyze the account of Hippolytus and give the reasons for taking a different view would require an article by itself, and cannot be undertaken here. But on the first point I will quote a writer who will not be suspected of an "apologetic" tendency, Matthew Arnold. He says: —

> It is true that the author of the *Philosophumena* [another name for the "Refutation of all Heresies" commonly ascribed to Hippolytus] sometimes mixes up the opinions of the master of a school with those of his followers, so that it is difficult to distinguish between them. But, if we take all doubtful cases of the kind and compare them with our present case, we shall find that it is not one of them. It is not true that here, where the name of Basileides has come just before, and where no mention of his son or of his disciples has intervened since, there is any such ambiguity as is found in other cases. It is not true that the author of the *Philosophumena* wields the *subjectless he says* in the random manner alleged, with no other formula for quotation both from the master and from the followers. In general, he uses the formula *according to them* (κατ' αὐτούς) when he quotes from the school, and the formula *he says* (φησί) when he gives the dicta of the master. And

in this particular case he manifestly quotes the dicta of Basileides, and no one who had not a theory to serve would ever dream of doubting it. Basileides, therefore, about the year 125 of our era, had before him the Fourth Gospel.*

On the second point, the view that Hippolytus as contrasted with Irenæus has given an account of the system of Basilides himself is the prevailing one among scholars : it is held, for example, by Jacobi, Bunsen, Baur, Hase, Uhlhorn, Möller, Mansel, Pressensé, and Dr. Hort. The principal representative of the opposite opinion is Hilgenfeld, with whom agree Lipsius, Volkmar, and Scholten.† Dr. Hort has discussed the matter very ably and fairly in his article *Basilides* in Smith and Wace's *Dictionary of Christian Biography;* and, so far as I can judge, his conclusions are sound.

In view of all the evidence, then, I think we have good reason for believing that the Gospel of John was one of a collection of Gospels, probably embracing our four, which Basilides and his followers received as authoritative about the year 125.

The first heretics described by Hippolytus are the Oriental Gnostics,— the Ophites, or Naassenes, and the Peratæ, a kindred sect. They are generally regarded as the earliest Gnostics. Hippolytus cites from their writings numerous quotations from the Gospel of John. ‡ But it is the view of many scholars that Hippolytus is really describing the opinions and quoting the writings of the later representatives of these sects. Not having investigated this point sufficiently, I shall argue only from what is undisputed.

Were I undertaking a full discussion of the external evidences of John's authorship of the Fourth Gospel, it would be necessary to consider here some questions about Papias,

---

* Matthew Arnold, *God and the Bible* (1875), p. 268 f., Eng. ed. See, to the same effect, Weizsäcker, *Untersuchungen* u. s. w., p. 232 ff. Compare Dr. Hort, art. *Basilides* in Smith and Wace's *Dict. of Christian Biog.*, i. 271, and Westcott, *Canon of the N.T.*, 4th ed., p. 288. On the other side, see Scholten, *Die ältesten Zeugnisse* u. s. w. (1867), p. 65 f.; *Sup. Rel.*, ii. 51, 7th ed., and the writers whom he there cites.

† The two most recent discussions are that by Jacobi, in Brieger's *Zeitschrift für Kirchengeschichte*, 1876-77, i. 481-544, and, on the other side, by Hilgenfeld, in his *Zeitschrift f. wiss. Theol.*, 1878, xxi. 228-250, where the literature of the subject is given pretty fully. Moeller, in a brief notice of the two articles (Brieger's *Zeitschrift*, 1877-78, ii. 422), adheres to his former view, *versus* Hilgenfeld.

‡ *Ref. Hær.* v. 7-9 (Naassenes), 12, 16, 17 (Peratæ).

and his use of the First Epistle of John, as reported by Eusebius; also the apparent reference to the First Epistle of John by Polycarp, and his relation to Irenæus; and, further, to notice the Ignatian Epistles, the "Testaments of the Twelve Patriarchs," and the Epistle to Diognetus. On the first two subjects, and on "The Silence of Eusebius," connected with the former, I would refer to the very able articles of Professor (now Bishop) Lightfoot in the *Contemporary Review*.* As to the Ignatian Epistles, their genuineness in any form is questionable, to say nothing of the state of the text, though the shorter Epistles may belong, in substance, to the middle of the second century; the "Testaments of the Twelve Patriarchs" are interpolated, and need a thoroughly critical edition; and the date of the Epistle to Diognetus is uncertain. In any event, I do not think the references to the Gospel of John in these writings are of great importance.

But to return to our proper subject. The use of the Gospel of John by the Gnostic sects, in the second century, affords a strong, it may seem decisive, argument for their genuineness. However ingeniously they might pervert its meaning, it is obvious to every intelligent reader that this Gospel is, in reality, diametrically opposed to the essential principles of Gnosticism. The Christian Fathers, in their contests with the Gnostics, found it an armory of weapons. Such being the case, let us suppose it to have been forged about the middle of the second century, in the heat of the Gnostic controversy. It was thus a book which the founders of the Gnostic sects, who flourished ten, twenty, or thirty years before, had never heard of. How is it possible, then, to explain the fact that their followers should have not only received it, but have received it, so far as appears, without question or discussion? It must have been received by the

---

* *Contemporary Review*, January, 1875, xxv. 169 ff., "The Silence of Eusebius"; May, 1875, p. 827 ff., "Polycarp of Smyrna"; August and October, 1875, xxvi. 377 ff., 828 ff., 'Papias of Hierapolis." On "the silence of Eusebius," see also Westcott, *Canon of the N. T.*, 4th ed., p. 229 f. With Lightfoot's article in the *Contemp. Review* for February, 1875, "The Ignatian Epistles," should be compared the Preface to *Supernatural Religion*, in the sixth and later editions of that work.

founders of these sects from the beginning; and we have no reason to distrust the testimony of Hippolytus to what is under these circumstances so probable, and is attested by other evidence. But, if received by the founders of these sects, it must have been received at the same time by the catholic Christians. They would not, at a later period, have taken the spurious work from the heretics with whom they were in controversy. It was then generally received, both by Gnostics and their opponents, between the years 120 and 130. What follows? It follows that the Gnostics of that date received it because they could not help it. They would not have admitted the authority of a book which could be reconciled with their doctrines only by the most forced interpretation, if they could have destroyed its authority by denying its genuineness. Its genuineness could then be easily ascertained. Ephesus was one of the principal cities of the Eastern world, the centre of extensive commerce, the metropolis of Asia Minor. Hundreds, if not thousands, of people were living who had known the Apostle John. The question whether he, the beloved disciple, had committed to writing his recollections of his Master's life and teaching, was one of the greatest interest. The fact of the reception of the Fourth Gospel as his work at so early a date, by parties so violently opposed to each other, proves that the evidence of its genuineness was decisive. This argument is further confirmed by the use of the Gospel by the opposing parties in the later Montanistic controversy, and in the disputes about the time of celebrating Easter.

THE last external evidence which I shall adduce in favor of the genuineness of the Gospel of John is of a very early date, being attached to the Gospel itself, and found in all the copies which have come down to us, whether in the original or in ancient versions. I refer to what is now numbered as the twenty-fifth verse, with the last half of the twenty-fourth, of the concluding chapter of the Gospel. The last three verses of the chapter read thus: "Hence this report spread among the brethren, that that disciple was not to die; yet Jesus did not say to him that he would not die; but, If I will that he remain till I come, what is that to thee? This is the disciple that testifieth concerning these things, and wrote these things." Here, I suppose, the author of the Gospel ended. The addition follows: "And *we* know that *his* testimony is true. And there are many other things that Jesus did, which, if they should be severally written, *I* do not think that the world itself would contain the books written."

In the words "And *we* know that *his* testimony is true," we manifestly have either a real or a forged attestation to the truth and genuineness of the Gospel. Suppose the Gospel written by an anonymous forger of the middle of the second century: what possible credit could he suppose would be given to it by an anonymous attestation like this? A forger with such a purpose would have named his pretended authority, and have represented the attestation as formally and solemnly given. The attestation, as it stands, clearly presupposes that the author (or authors) of it was known to those who first received the copy of the Gospel containing it.

What view, then, are we to take of it? The following supposition, which I give in the words of Mr. Norton, affords an easy and natural explanation, and, so far as I can see, the only plausible explanation of the phenomena. Mr. Norton says:—

According to ancient accounts, St. John wrote his Gospel at Ephesus, over the church in which city he presided during the latter part of his long life. It is not improbable that, before his death, its circulation had been confined to the members of that church. Hence copies of it would be afterwards obtained; and the copy provided for transcription was, we may suppose, accompanied by the strong attestation which we now find, given by the church, or the elders of the church, to their full faith in the accounts which it contained, and by the concluding remark, made by the writer of this attestation in his own person.*

The style of this addition, it is further to be observed,

---

*Norton, *Genuineness of the Gospels*, 2d ed., vol. i., Addit. Notes, p. xcv. f.

differs from that of the writer of the Gospel. It was probably first written a little separate from the text, and afterwards became incorporated with it by a natural mistake of transcribers. According to Tischendorf, the last verse of this Gospel in the Codex Sinaiticus is written in a different hand from the preceding, though by a contemporary scribe. He accordingly rejects it as not having belonged to the Gospel as it was originally written. Tregelles does not agree with him on the palæographical question.

The passage we have been considering suggests various questions and remarks, but cannot be further treated here. I will only refer to the recent commentaries of Godet and Westcott, and end abruptly the present discussion, which has already extended to a far greater length than was originally intended.

Note A. (See p. 22.)

ON THE QUOTATIONS OF MATT. xi. 27 (*comp.* LUKE x. 22) IN THE WRITINGS OF THE CHRISTIAN FATHERS.

Justin Martyr (*Dial.* c. 100) quotes the following as "written in the Gospel": "All things have been delivered (παραδέδοται) to me by the Father; and no one *knoweth* (γινώσκει) the Father save the Son, neither [knoweth any one] the Son save the Father, and they to whomsoever the Son may reveal him" (οἷς ἂν ὁ υἱὸς ἀποκαλύψῃ). In the *Apology* (c. 63) he quotes the passage twice, thus: "No one *knew* (or "hath known," ἔγνω) the Father save the Son, neither [knoweth any one] the Son save the Father, and they to whomsoever the Son may reveal him"; the order of the words, however, varying in the last clause, in which ὁ υἱός stands once after ἀποκαλύψῃ.

It is unnecessary to quote the corresponding passages in our Gospels in full, as the reader can readily turn to them. The variations of Justin are, (1) the use of the perfect (παραδέδοται), "have been delivered," instead of the aorist (παρεδόθη), strictly, "were delivered," though our idiom often requires the aorist to be translated by the perfect; (2) "*the* Father" for "*my* Father" (omitting μου); (3) the use, in two out of three instances, of the aorist ἔγνω, "knew," or "hath known," instead of the present γινώσκει (this is the word used by Luke; Matthew has ἐπιγινώσκει); (4) the transposition of the two principal clauses; (5) the omission of τις ἐπιγινώσκει, "knoweth any one," in the second clause, if we compare Matthew, or the substitution of "the Father" and "the Son" for "who the Father is" and "who the Son is," if we compare Luke; (6) the use of the plural (οἷς ἂν), "*they* to whomsoever," instead of the singular (ᾧ ἂν), "*he* to whomsoever"; and (7) the substitution of "may reveal" (ἀποκαλύψῃ) for "may will to reveal" (βούληται ἀποκαλύψαι).

The author of *Supernatural Religion* devotes more than ten pages to this passage (vol. i. pp. 401-412, 7th ed.), which he regards as of great importance, and insists, on the ground of these variations, that Justin could not have taken it from our Gospels. To follow him step by step would be tedious. His fundamental error is the assertion that "the peculiar form of the quotation in Justin" (here he refers especially to the variations numbered 3 and 4, above) "occurred in what came to be considered heretical Gospels, and constituted the basis of important Gnostic doctrines" (p. 403). Again, "Here we have the exact quotation twice made by Justin, with the ἔγνω and the same order, set forth as the reading of the Gospels of the Marcosians and other sects, and the highest testimony to their system" (pp. 406, 407). Yet again, "Irenæus states with equal distinctness that Gospels used by Gnostic sects had the reading of Justin" (p. 411). Now Irenæus nowhere states any such thing. Irenæus nowhere speaks, nor does any other ancient writer, of a Gospel of the Marcosians. If this sect had set up a Gospel (*i.e.*, a history of Christ's ministry) of its own, in opposition to the Four Gospels received by the whole Christian Church in the time of Irenæus, we should have had unequivocal evidence of the fact. The denunciations of Marcion for mutilating the Gospel of Luke show how such a work would have been treated. Irenæus is indignant that the Valentinians should give to "a recent work of their own composition" the name of "The Gospel of the Truth" or "The True Gospel" (*Hær.* iii. 11. § 9); but this was in all probability a doctrinal or speculative, not an historical work.* The Valentinians received our four Gospels without controversy, and argued from them in support of their doctrines as best they could. (See Irenæus, *Hær.* i. cc. 7, 8, for numerous examples of their arguments from the Gospels; and compare iii. 11. § 7; 12. § 12; and Tertull. *Præscr.* c. 38.)

Correcting this fundamental error of the author of *Supernatural Religion*, the facts which he himself states respecting the various forms in which this passage is quoted by writers who unquestionably used our four Gospels as their sole or main authority, are sufficient to show the groundlessness of his conclusion. But for the sake of illustrating the freedom of the Christian Fathers in quotation, and the falsity of the premises on which this writer reasons, I will exhibit the facts somewhat more fully than they have been presented elsewhere, though the quotations of this passage have been elaborately discussed by Credner,† Semisch,‡ Hilgenfeld,|| Volckmar,** and Westcott.†† Of these discussions those by Semisch and Volckmar are particularly valuable.

I will now notice all the variations of Justin from the text of our Gospels in this passage (see above), comparing them with those found in other writers. The two most important (Nos. 3 and 4) will be examined last.

1. παραδέδοται for παρεδόθη is wholly unimportant. It is found in Luke x. 22

---

* See Norton, *Genuineness of the Gospels*, iii. 227 f.; Westcott, *Canon of the N. T.*, 4th ed., p. 297 f.; Lipsius, art. *Gospels, Apocryphal*, in Smith and Wace's *Dict. of Christian Biog.*, vol. ii. (1880), p. 717.

† *Beiträge zur Einl. in die biblischen Schriften* (1832), i. pp. 248-251.

‡ *Die apostol. Denkwürdigkeiten des Märt. Justinus* (1848), pp. 364-370.

|| *Kritische Untersuchungen über die Evangelien Justin's*, u. s. w. (1850), pp. 201-206.

** *Das Evang. Marcions* (1852), pp. 75-80. I follow the title in spelling "Volckmar."

†† *Canon of the N. T.*, 4th ed. (1875), pp. 133-135. See also Sanday, *The Gospels in the Second Century*, pp. 132, 133, and chaps. ii., iv., vi.

in the uncial MSS. K and Π, the cursives 60, 253, p^scr, w^scr, three of Colbert's MSS. (see Wetstein *in loc.* and his Prolegom. p. 48), and in HIPPOLYTUS (*Noët.* c. 6), not heretofore noticed.

2. "*The* Father" for "*my* Father," μου being omitted, is equally trivial; so in the Sinaitic MS. and the cursive 71 in Matthew, and in Luke the Codex Bezæ (D), with some of the best MSS. of the Old Latin and Vulgate versions, and other authorities (see Tischendorf), also HIPPOLYTUS as above.

5. The omission of τις ἐπιγινώσκει or its equivalent in the second clause is found in the citation of the MARCOSIANS in Irenæus (i. 20. § 3), other GNOSTICS in Irenæus (iv. 6. § 1), and in IRENÆUS himself three times (ii. 6. § 1; iv. 6. §§ 3, 7, but *not* § 1). It occurs twice in CLEMENT OF ALEXANDRIA (*Pæd.* i. 9, p. 150 ed. Potter; *Strom.* i. 28, p. 425), once in ORIGEN (*Cels.* vi. 17, p. 643), once in ATHANASIUS (*Orat. cont. Arian.* iii. c. 46, p. 596), 6 times in EPIPHANIUS (*Ancor.* c. 67, p. 71, repeated *Hær.* lxxiv. 4, p. 891; c. 73, p. 78, repeated *Hær.* lxxiv. 10, p. 898; and *Hær.* lxiv. 9, p. 643; lxxvi. 7, 29, 32, pp. 943, 977, 981); once in CHRYSOSTOM (*In Joan. Hom.* lx. §1, Opp. viii. 353 (404) A, ed. Montf.), once in PSEUDO-CYRIL (*De Trin.* c. 1), once in MAXIMUS CONFESSOR (*Schol. in* Dion. Areop. *de div. Nom.* c. 1. § 2, in Migne, *Patrol. Gr.* iv. 189), once in JOANNES DAMASCENUS (*De Fide Orth.* i. 1) and twice in GEORGIUS PACHYMERES (*Paraphr. in* Dion. Areop. *de div. Nom.* c. 1, §1, and *de myst. Theol.* c. 5; Migne, iii. 613, 1061). It is noticeable that the CLEMENTINE HOMILIES (xvii. 4; xviii. 4, 13 *bis*, 20) do not here agree with Justin.

6. There is no difference between οἷς ἄν, "*they* to whomsoever," and ᾧ ἄν (or ἐάν), "*he* to whomsoever," so far as the sense is concerned. The plural, which Justin uses, is found in the CLEMENTINE HOMILIES 5 times (xvii. 4; xviii. 4, 13 *bis*, 20), and IRENÆUS 5 times (*Hær.* ii. 6. § 1; iv. 6.§§ 3, 4, 7, and so the Syriac; 7. § 3). The singular is used in the citations given by Irenæus from the MARCOSIANS (i. 20. § 3) and "those who would be wiser than the Apostles," as well as in his own express quotation from Matthew (*Hær.* iv. 6. § 1); and so by the Christian Fathers generally.

7. The next variation (οἷς ἂν ὁ υἱὸς ἀποκαλύψῃ for βούληται ἀποκαλύψαι) is a natural shortening of the expression, which we find in the citation of the MARCOSIANS (Iren. i. 20. § 3) and in IRENÆUS himself 5 times (ii. 6. § 1; iv. 6. §§ 3, 4, 7, and so the Syriac; 7. § 3); in TERTULLIAN twice (*Marc.* iv. 25; *Præscr.* c. 21), and perhaps in Marcion's mutilated Luke; in CLEMENT OF ALEXANDRIA 5 times (*Cohort.* i. 10, p. 10; *Pæd.* I. 5, p.109; *Strom.* i. 28, p.425; v. 13, p. 697; vii. 18, p. 901;—*Quis dives*, etc., c. 8, p. 939, is a mere allusion); ORIGEN 4 times (*Cels.* vi. 17, p. 643; vii. 44, p.726; *in Joan.* tom. i. c. 42, p. 45: tom. xxxii. c. 18, p. 450); the SYNOD OF ANTIOCH against Paul of Samosata (Routh, *Rell. sacræ*, ed. alt. iii. 290); EUSEBIUS or MARCELLUS in Eusebius 3 times (*Eccl. Theol.* i. 15, 16, pp. 76^c, 77^d, ἀποκαλύψει; *Ecl. proph.* i. 12 [Migne, *Patrol. Gr.* xxii. col. 1065], ἀποκαλύψῃ); ATHANASIUS 4 or 5 times (*Decret. Nic. Syn.* c. 12, Opp. i. 218 ed. Bened.; *Orat. cont. Arian.* i. c. 12, p. 416; c. 39, p. 443; iii. c. 46, p. 596, in the best MSS.; *Serm. maj. de Fide*, c. 27, in Montf. *Coll. nova*, ii. 14); CYRIL OF JERUSALEM twice (*Cat.* vi. 6; x. 1); EPIPHANIUS 4 times (*Ancor.* c. 67, p. 71, repeated *Hær.* lxxiv. 4, p. 891, but here ἀποκαλύπτει or -τῃ; *Hær.* lxv. 6, p. 613; and without ὁ υἱός, *Hær.* lxxvi. 7, p. 943; c. 29, p. 977); BASIL THE GREAT (*Adv. Eunom.* v. Opp. i. 311 (441) A); CYRIL OF ALEXANDRIA 3 times *Thes.* Opp. v. 131, 149; *Cont. Julian.* viii. Opp. vi. b. p. 270).

All of these variations are obviously unimportant, and natural in quoting from memory, and the extent to which they occur in writers who unquestionably used our Gospels as their sole or main authority shows that their occurrence in Justin affords no ground for supposing that he did not also so use them.

We will then turn our attention to the two variations on which the main stress is laid by the author of *Supernatural Religion*. He greatly exaggerates their importance, and neglects an obvious explanation of their origin.

3. We find ἔγνω, "knew," or "hath known," for γινώσκει or ἐπιγινώσκει, in the CLEMENTINE HOMILIES 6 times (xvii. 4; xviii. 4, 11, 13 *bis*, 20), and once apparently in the RECOGNITIONS (ii. 47, *novit*); twice in TERTULLIAN (*Adv. Marc.* ii. 27; *Præscr.* c. 21); in CLEMENT OF ALEXANDRIA 6 times (*Cohort.* i. 10, p. 10; *Pæd.* i. 5, p. 109; i. 8, p. 142; i. 9, p. 150; *Strom.* i. 28, p. 425; v. 13, p. 697; — once the present, γινώσκει, *Strom.* vii. 18, p. 901; and once, in a mere allusion, ἐπιγινώσκει, *Quis dives*, etc., c. 8, p. 939); ORIGEN uniformly, 10 times (*Opp.* i. 440, 643, 726; ii. 537; iv. 45, 234, 284, 315, 450 *bis*), and in the Latin version of his writings of which the Greek is lost *novit* is used 10 times, including *Opp.* iii. 58, where *novit* is used for Matthew and *scit* for Luke; *scit* occurs also *Opp.* iv. 515. The SYNOD OF ANTIOCH *versus* Paul of Samosata has it once (Routh, *Rell. sacræ*, iii. 290); ALEXANDER OF ALEXANDRIA once (*Epist. ad Alex.* c. 5, Migne, *Patr. Gr.* xviii. 556); EUSEBIUS 6 times (*Eccl. Theol.* i. 12, 16, pp. 72ᵉ, 77ᵈ; *Dem. Evang.* iv. 3, v. 1, pp. 149ᶜ, 216ᵈ; *Ecl. proph.* i. 12, Migne xxii. 1065; *Hist. Eccl.* i. 2. §2); DIDYMUS OF ALEXANDRIA once (*De Trin.* ii. 5, p. 142); EPIPHANIUS twice (*Hær.* lxv. 6, p. 613; lxxiv. 10, p. 898).— Of these writers, Alexander has οἶδε once; Eusebius γινώσκει or ἐπιγινώσκει 3 times, Didymus γινώσκει followed by ἐπιγινώσκει 3 times, Epiphanius has οἶδε 9 or 10 times, and it is found also in Basil, Chrysostom, and Cyril of Alexandria. Marcellus in Eusebius (*Eccl. Theol.* i. 15, 16, pp. 76ᵉ, 78ᵈ) wavers between οἶδε (twice) and γινώσκει or ἐπιγινώσκει (once), and perhaps ἔγνω (c. 16, p. 77ᵈ).

4. We find the *transposition* of the clauses, "No one knoweth [*or* knew] the Father" coming first, in one MS. in Matthew (Matthæi's d) and two in Luke (the uncial U and i ˢᶜʳ), in the *Diatessaron* of TATIAN as its text is given in the Armenian version of Ephraem's Commentary upon it, translated into Latin by Aucher, and published by G. Moesinger (*Evangelii concordantis Expositio*, etc., Venet. 1876),* the CLEMENTINE HOMILIES 5 times (xvii. 4; xviii. 4, 13 *bis*, 20), the MARCOSIANS in Irenæus (i. 20. §3), other GNOSTICS in Irenæus (iv. 6. §1), and IRENÆUS himself (ii. 6. §1; iv. 6. §3, *versus* §1 and §7, *Lat.*, but here a Syriac version represented by a MS. of the 6th century, gives the transposed form; see Harvey's Irenæus, ii. 443), TERTULLIAN once (*Adv. Marc.* iv. 25), ORIGEN once (*De Princip.* ii. 6. §1, Opp. i. 89, in a Latin version), the SYNOD OF ANTIOCH against Paul of Samosata (as cited above), the MARCIONITE in PSEUDO-ORIG. *Dial. de recta in Deum fide*, sect. i. Opp. i. 817); EUSEBIUS 4 times (*Eccl. Theol.* i. 12; *Dem. Evang.* iv. 3, v. 1; *Hist. Eccl.* i. 2. §2), ALEXANDER OF ALEXANDRIA once (*Epist. ad Alex.* c. 12, Migne xviii. 565); ATHANASIUS twice (*In illud, Omnia mihi tradita sunt*, c. 5, Opp. i. 107; *Serm. maj. de Fide*, c. 27, in Montf. *Coll. nova*, ii. 14), DIDYMUS once (*De Trin.* i. 26, p. 72), EPIPHANIUS 7 times, or 9 times if the passages transferred from the *Ancoratus* are reckoned (*Opp.* i. 766, 891, 898, 977, 981; ii. 16, 19, 67, 73), CHRYSOSTOM once (*In*

---

* This reads (pp. 117, 216), "Nemo novit Patrem nisi Filius, et nemo novit Filium nisi Pater."

Ascens., etc., c. 14, Opp. iii. 771 (931) ed. Montf.), PSEUDO-CYRIL OF ALEXANDRIA once (*De Trin.* c. 1, Opp. vi. c. p. 1), PSEUDO-CAESARIUS twice (*Dial.* i. *resp.* 3 and 20, in Migne xxxviii. 861, 877), MAXIMUS CONFESSOR once (*Schol. in* Dion. Areop. *de div. Nom.* c. 1. §2, in Migne iv. 189), JOANNES DAMASCENUS once (*De Fide Orth.* i. 1), and GEORGIUS PACHYMERES once (*Paraphr. in* Dion. Areop. *de div. Nom.* c. 1. §1, in Migne iii. 613).

This transposition is found in MS. b of the Old Latin, and some of the Latin Fathers, *e.g.*, Phæbadius (*Cont. Arian.* c. 10); and most MSS. of the Old Latin, and the Vulgate, read *novit* in Matthew instead of *scit* or *cognoscit*, which they have in Luke; but it is not worth while to explore this territory here.

It is manifest from this presentation of the facts that the variations to which the author of *Supernatural Religion* attaches so much importance,— the transposition of the clauses, and the use of the past tense for the present,— being not peculiar to Justin and the heretics, but found in a multitude of the Christian Fathers, can afford no proof or presumption that the source of his quotation was not our present Gospels — that he does not use in making it (*Dial.* c. 100) the term "the Gospel" in the same sense in which it is used by his later contemporaries. It indeed seems probable that the reading ἔγνω, though not in the MSS. which have come down to us, had already found its way into some MSS. of the second century, particularly in Matthew. Its almost uniform occurrence in the numerous citations of the passage by Clement of Alexandria and Origen, and the reading of the Old Latin MSS. and of the Vulgate, favor this view. The transposition of the clauses may also have been found in some MSS. of that date, as we even now find its existence in several manuscripts. But it is not necessary to suppose this; the Fathers, in quoting, make such transpositions with great freedom. The stress laid on the transposition in *Supernatural Religion* is very extravagant. It did not affect the sense, but merely made more prominent the knowledge and the revelation of the Father by Christ. The importance of the change from the present tense to the past is also preposterously exaggerated. It merely expressed more distinctly what the present implied. Further, these variations admit of an easy explanation. In preaching Christianity to unbelievers, special emphasis would be laid on the fact that Christ had come to give men a true knowledge of God, of God in his paternal character. The transposition of the clauses in quoting this striking passage, which must have been often quoted, would thus be very natural; and so would be the change from the present tense to the past. The Gnostics, moreover, regarding the God of the Old Testament as an inferior and imperfect being, maintained that the true God, the Supreme, had been wholly unknown to men before he was revealed by Christ. They would, therefore, naturally quote the passage in the same way; and the variation at an early period would become wide-spread. That Irenæus should notice a difference between the form in which the Gnostics quoted the text and that which he found in his own copy of the Gospels is not strange; but there is nothing in what he says which implies that it was anything more than a various reading or corruption of the text of Matthew or Luke; he nowhere charges the Gnostics with taking it from Gospels peculiar to themselves. It is their *interpretation* of the passage rather than their text which he combats. The change of order further occurs frequently in writers who are treating of the divinity of Christ, as Athanasius, Didymus, Epiphanius. Here the occasion seems to have been that the fact that Christ alone fully knew the

Father was regarded as proving his deity, and the transposition of the clauses gave special prominence to that fact. Another occasion was the circumstance that when the Father and the Son are mentioned together in the New Testament, the name of the Father commonly stands first; and the transposition was the more natural in the present case, because, as Semisch remarks, the word "Father" immediately precedes.

In this statement, I have only exhibited those variations in the quotation of this text by the Fathers which correspond with those of Justin. These give a very inadequate idea of the extraordinary variety of forms in which the passage appears. I will simply observe, by way of specimen, that, while Eusebius quotes the passage at least eleven times, none of his quotations verbally agree. (See *Cont. Marcel.* i. 1, p. 6^a; *Eccl. Theol.* i. 12, 15, 16 *bis*, 20, pp. 72^c, 76^e, 77^d, 78^a, 88^d; *Dem. Evang.* iv. 3, v. 1, pp. 149^e, 216^d; *Comm. in Ps.* cx.; *Ecl. proph.* i. 12; *Hist. Eccl.* i. 2. § 2.) The two quotations which he introduces from Marcellus (*Eccl. Theol.* i. 15 and 16) present a still different form. In three of Eusebius's quotations for εἰ μὴ ὁ πατήρ he reads εἰ μὴ ὁ μόνος γεννήσας αὐτὸν πατήρ (*Eccl. Theol.* i. 12, p. 72^e; *Dem. Evang.* iv. 3, p. 149^e; and *Hist. Eccl.* i. 2. § 2). If this were found in Justin Martyr, it would be insisted that it must have come from some apocryphal Gospel, and the triple recurrence would be thought to prove it.* The variations in Epiphanius, who also quotes the passage eleven times (not counting the transfers from the *Ancoratus*), are perhaps equally remarkable. PSEUDO-CÆSARIUS quotes it thus (*Dial.* i. *resp.* 3): Οὐδεὶς γὰρ οἶδε τὸν πατέρα εἰ μὴ ὁ υἱός, οὐδὲ τὸν υἱόν τις ἐπίσταται εἰ μὴ ὁ πατήρ. But the false premises from which the author of *Supernatural Religion* reasons have been sufficiently illustrated.

This Note is too long to allow the discussion of some points which need a fuller treatment. I will only call attention to the fact that in the list of passages *in our Gospels* which Irenæus (i. 20. § 2) represents the Marcosians as perverting, there is one which presents a difficulty, and which some have supposed to be taken from an apocryphal Gospel. As it stands, the text is corrupt, and the passage makes no sense. Mr. Norton in the *first edition* of his *Genuineness of the Gospels* (1837), vol. i. Addit. Notes, p. ccxlii., has given a plausible conjectural emendation of the text in Irenæus, which serves to clear up the difficulty. For the πολλάκις ἐπεθύμησα of Irenæus he would read πολλοὶ καὶ ἐπεθύμησαν, for δεῖν, εἶναι (so the old Latin version), and for διὰ τοῦ ἑνός, διὰ τοῦ ἐροῦντος. The passage then becomes a modification of Matt. xiii. 17. Dr. Westcott (*Canon of the N. T.*, 4th ed., p. 306) proposes ἐπεθύμησαν for ἐπεθύμησα, without being aware that his conjecture had been anticipated. But that change alone does not restore sense to the passage. The masterly review of Credner's hypothesis that Justin's Memoirs were the so-called "Gospel according to Peter," which contains Mr. Norton's emendation to which I have referred, was not reprinted in the *second* edition of his work. It seemed to me, therefore, worth while to notice it here.

---

* Compare *Supernatural Religion*, i. 341.

NOTE B. (See p. 23.)

ON THE TITLE, "MEMOIRS BY *the* APOSTLES."

In regard to the use of the article here, it may be well to notice the points made by Hilgenfeld, perhaps the ablest and the fairest of the German critics who regard some apocryphal Gospel or Gospels as the chief source of Justin's quotations. His book is certainly the most valuable which has appeared on that side of the question.*

In the important passage (*Dial.* c. 103), in which Justin says, "In the Memoirs which I affirm to have been composed by the Apostles of Christ and their companions (ἅ φημι ὑπὸ τῶν ἀποστόλων αὐτοῦ καὶ τῶν ἐκείνοις παρακολουθησάντων συντετάχθαι), it is written that sweat, like drops of blood [*or* "clots," θρόμβοι], flowed from him while he was praying" (comp. Luke xxii. 44), and which Semisch very naturally compares, as regards its description of the Gospels, with a striking passage of Tertullian,† Hilgenfeld insists —

(1) That the article denotes "the collective body" (*die Gesammtheit*) of the Apostles and their companions.

(2) "The Memoirs by the Apostles" is the phrase generally used by Justin. This might indeed be justified by the fact that the Gospels of Mark and Luke were regarded as founded on the direct communications of Apostles or sanctioned by them; but this, Hilgenfeld says, is giving up the sharp distinction between the Gospels as written two of them by Apostles and two by Apostolic men.

(3) The fact that Justin appeals to the "Memoirs by the *Apostles*" for incidents, like the visit of the Magi, which are recorded by only *one* apostle, "shows clearly the utter indefiniteness of this form of expression." ‡ "Manifestly, that single passage," namely, the one quoted above (*Dial.* c. 103), "must be explained in accordance with Justin's general use of language."

Let us examine these points. As to (1), the supposition that Justin conceived of his "Memoirs" as "composed" or "written" — these are the words he uses — by "the collective body" of the Apostles of Christ and "the collective body" of their companions is a simple absurdity.

(2) and (3). For Justin's purpose, it was important, and it was sufficient, to represent the "Memoirs" to which he appealed as resting on the authority of the Apostles. But in one place he has described them more particularly; and it is simply reasonable to say that the more general expression should be interpreted in accordance with the precise description, and not, as Hilgenfeld strangely contends, the reverse.

---

*See his *Kritische Untersuchungen über die Evangelien Justin's, der clementinischen Homilien und Marcion's* (Halle, 1850), p. 13 ff.

†*Adv. Marc.* iv. 2: Constituimus inprimis evangelicum instrumentum apostolos auctores habere.... Si et apostolicos, non tamen solos, sed cum apostolis et post apostolos.... Denique nobis fidem ex apostolis Ioannes et Matthæus insinuant, ex apostolicis Lucas et Marcus instaurant.

‡ Hilgenfeld also refers to Justin (*Dial.* c. 101, p. 328, comp. *Apol.* i. 38) for a passage relating to the mocking of Christ at the crucifixion, which Justin, referring to the "Memoirs," describes "in a form," as he conceives, "essentially differing from all our canonical Gospels." To me it appears that the agreement is essential, and the difference of slight importance and easily explained; but to discuss the matter here would be out of place, and would carry us too far.

(3) The fact that Justin appeals to the "Memoirs by the Apostles" for an incident which is related by only *one* Apostle is readily explained by the fact that he gives this title to the Gospels considered *collectively*, just as he once designates them as εὐαγγέλια, "Gospels," and twice as τὸ εὐαγγέλιον, "the Gospel." The usage of the Christian Fathers in quoting is entirely analogous. They constantly cite passages as contained "in the Gospels" which are found only in *one* Gospel, simply because "the Gospels" was a term used interchangeably with "the Gospel," to denote the four Gospels conceived of as one book. For examples of this use of the plural, see the note to p. 22. To the instances there given, many might easily be added.

Hilgenfeld, in support of his view of the article here, cites the language of Justin where, in speaking of the new birth, he says, "And the reason for this we have learned from *the* Apostles" (*Apol.* i. 61). Here it seems to me not improbable that Justin had in mind the language of Christ as recorded by the Apostles John and Matthew in John iii. 6, 7, and Matt. xviii. 3, 4. That he had *no* particular Apostles or apostolic writings in view — that by "the Apostles" he meant vaguely "the collective body of the Apostles" does not appear likely. The statement must have been founded on something which he had read *somewhere*.

NOTE C. (See p. 78.)

JUSTIN MARTYR AND THE "GOSPEL ACCORDING TO THE HEBREWS."

After remarking that the "Gospel according to the Hebrews" was "almost universally regarded in the first centuries as the Hebrew original of our canonical Gospel of St. Matthew," that Greek versions of it "must have existed at a very early date," and that "at various times and in different circles it took very different shapes," Lipsius observes: "The fragments preserved in the Greek by Epiphanius betray very clearly their dependence on our canonical Gospels. ... The Aramaic fragments also contain much that can be explained and understood only on the hypothesis that it is a recasting of the canonical text.... The narrative of our Lord's baptism (Epiphan. *Hær.* xxx. 13), with its *threefold* voice from heaven, is evidently a more recent combination of older texts, of which the first is found in the Gospels of St. Mark and St. Luke; the second in the text of the Cambridge *Cod. Bezæ* at St. Luke iii. 22, in Justin Martyr (*Dial. c. Tryphon.* 88, 103), and Clemens Alexandrinus (*Pædag.* i. 6, p. 113, Potter); the third in our canonical Gospel of St. Matthew. And this very narrative may suffice to prove that the so-called 'Hebrew' text preserved by St. Jerome is by no means preferable to that of our canonical Gospel of St. Matthew, and even less original than the Greek text quoted by Epiphanius."* "The attempt to prove that Justin Martyr and the Clementine Homilies had one extra-canonical

---

* Smith and Wace's *Dict. of Christian Biog.*, vol. ii. (1880), p. 710. Many illustrations are here given of the fact that most of the quotations which have come down to us from the "Gospel of the Hebrews" belong to a later period, and represent a later stage of theological development, than our canonical Gospels. Mangold agrees with Lipsius. See the note in his edition of Bleek's *Einleitung in das N. T.*, 3º Aufl. (1875), p. 132 f. Dr. E. A. Abbott, art. *Gospels* in the ninth ed. of the Encyclopædia Britannica (x. 818, note), takes the same view. He finds no evidence that Justin Martyr made any use of the Gospel according to the Hebrews.

authority common to them both, either in the *Gospel of the Hebrews* or in the *Gospel of St. Peter*, ... has altogether failed. It is only in the rarest cases that they literally agree in their deviations from the text of our Gospels; they differ in their citations as much, for the most part, one from the other as they do from the text of the synoptical evangelists, even in such cases when one or the other repeatedly quotes the same passage, and each time in the same words. Only in very few cases is the derivation from the *Gospel of the Hebrews* probable, as in the saying concerning the new birth (Justin M. *Apol.* i. 61; Clem. *Homilies*, xi. 26; *Recogn.* vi. 9); ... in most cases ... it is quite enough to assume that the quotations were made from memory, and so account for the involuntary confusion of evangelic texts." (*Ibid.* p. 712.)

Mr. E. B. Nicholson, in his elaborate work on the Gospel according to the Hebrews (Lond. 1879), comes to the conclusion that "there are no proofs that Justin used the Gospel according to the Hebrews at all" (p. 135). He also observes, "There is no reason to suppose that the authorship of the Gospel according to the Hebrews was attributed to the Apostles generally in the 2d or even the 3d cent. Irenæus calls it simply 'that Gospel which is according to Matthew'" (p. 134).

Holtzmann in the eighth volume of Bunsen's *Bibelwerk* (1866) discusses at length the subject of apocryphal Gospels. He comes to the conclusion that the "Gospel of the Hebrews" or "of the Nazarenes" was an Aramaic redaction (*Bearbeitung*) of our Matthew, executed in an exclusively Jewish-Christian spirit, making some use of Jewish-Christian traditions, but presupposing the Synoptic and the Pauline literature. It was probably made in Palestine for the Jewish-Christian churches some time in the second century (p. 547). The Gospel of the Ebionites, for our knowledge of which we have to depend almost wholly on Epiphanius, a very untrustworthy writer, Holtzmann regards as "a Greek recasting (*Ueberarbeitung*) of the Synoptic Gospels, with peculiar Jewish-Christian traditions and theosophic additions" (p. 553).

Professor Drummond, using Kirchhofer's *Quellensammlung*, has compared the twenty-two fragments of the Gospel according to the Hebrews there collected (including those of the Gospel of the Ebionites) with Justin's citations from or references to the Gospels, of which he finds about one hundred and seventy. I give his result: —

"With an apparent exception to be noticed presently, not one of the twenty-two quotations from the lost Gospel is found among these one hundred and seventy. But this is not all. While thirteen deal with matters not referred to in Justin, nine admit of comparison; and in these nine instances not only does Justin omit everything that is characteristic of the Hebrew Gospel, but in some points he distinctly differs from it, and agrees with the canonical Gospels. There is an apparent exception. Justin quotes the voice from heaven at the baptism in this form, 'Thou art my son; this day have I begotten thee.' 'This day have I begotten thee' is also in the Ebionite Gospel;[*] but there it is awkwardly appended to a second saying, thus: 'Thou art my beloved Son; in thee was I well pleased; and again, This day have I begotten thee'; — so that the passage is quite different from Justin's, and has the appearance of being a later patchwork. Justin's form of quotation is still the reading of the Codex

---

[*] See Epiphanius, *Hær.* xxx. 13; Nicholson, *The Gospel according to the Hebrews*, p. 40 ff. — E. A.

Bezæ in Luke, and, according to Augustine, was found in good MSS., though it was said not to be in the older ones. (See Tischend. in loco.) * One other passage is appealed to. Justin says that, when Jesus *went down upon the water*, a fire was kindled in the Jordan,—πῦρ ἀνήφθη ἐν τῷ Ἰορδάνῃ. The Ebionite Gospel relates that, when Jesus *came up from the water*, immediately a great light shone round the place,— εὐθὺς περιέλαμψε τὸν τόπον φῶς μέγα. This fact is, I believe, the main proof that Justin used the Gospel according to the Hebrews, and that we may therefore have recourse to it, whenever he differs verbally from the existing Gospels. Considering that the events recorded are not the same, that they are said to have happened at different times, and that the two quotations do not agree with one another in a single word, this argument cannot be considered very convincing, even by those who do not require perfect verbal accuracy in order to identify a quotation. But, further, the author of the anonymous Liber de Rebaptismate says that this event was related in an heretical work entitled Pauli Prædicatio, and that it was not found in any Gospel: 'Item cum baptizaretur, ignem super aquam esse visum; quod in evangelio nullo est scriptum.' (Routh, Rel. Sac. v. pp. 325, 326 [c. 14, Routh; c. 17, Hartel.]) Of course the latter statement may refer only to the canonical Gospels."† To this it may be added that a comparison of the fuller collection of fragments of "the Gospel according to the Hebrews" given by Hilgenfeld or Nicholson (the latter makes out a list of thirty-three fragments) would be still less favorable to the supposition that Justin made use of this Gospel.

In the quotations which I have given from these independent writers, I have not attempted to set forth in full their views of the relation of the original Hebrew Gospel to our Greek Matthew, still less my own; but enough has been said to show how little evidence there is that the "Gospel of the Hebrews" in one form or another either constituted Justin's "Memoirs," or was the principal source from which he drew his knowledge of the life of Christ. While I find nothing like *proof* that Justin made use of any apocryphal Gospel, the question whether he may in a few instances have done so is wholly unimportant. Such a use would not in his case, any more than in that of the later Fathers, as Clement of Alexandria, Origen, Jerome, imply that he placed such a work on a level with our four Gospels.

The notion that Justin used mainly the "Gospel according to Peter," which is assumed, absolutely without evidence, to have been a form of the "Gospel according to the Hebrews," rests almost wholly on the hypothesis, for which there is also not a particle of evidence, that this Gospel was mainly used by the

---

* It is the reading also (in Luke iii. 22) of the best MSS. of the old Latin version or versions, of Clement of Alexandria, Methodius, Lactantius, Juvencus, Hilary of Poitiers in several places, Hilary the deacon (if he is the author of *Quæstiones Vet. et Nov. Test.*), and Faustus the Manichæan; and Augustine quotes it once without remark. It seems to be presupposed in the Apostolical Constitutions (ii. 32); see the note of Cotelier *in loc.* It is altogether probable therefore that Justin found it in his MS. of Luke. The words (from Ps. ii. 7) being repeatedly applied to Christ in the N.T. (Acts xiii. 33; Heb. i. 5; v. 5), the substitution might easily occur through confusion of memory, or from the words having been noted in the margin of MSS. — E. A.

† *Theol. Review*, October, 1875, xii. 482 f., note. The *Liber de Rebaptismate* is usually published with the works of Cyprian.

author of the Clementine Homilies. The agreement between certain quotations of Justin and those found in the Clementine Homilies in their variations from the text of our Gospels is supposed to prove that Justin and Clement drew from a common source; namely, this "Gospel according to Peter," from which they are then imagined to have derived the great body of their citations. The facts stated in the quotation I have given above from Lipsius, who has expressed himself none too strongly, are enough to show the baselessness of this hypothesis; but it may be well to say a few words about the alleged agreement in *five* quotations between Justin and the Clementines in their variations from the text of our Gospels. These are all that have been or can be adduced in argument with the least plausibility. The two most remarkable of them, namely, Matt. xi. 27 (par. with Luke x. 22) and John iii. 3–5, have already been fully discussed.* In two of the three remaining cases, an examination of the various readings in Tischendorf's last critical edition of the Greek Testament (1869–72), and of the parallels in the Christian Fathers cited by Semisch and others, will show at once the utter worthlessness of the argument. †

The last example alone requires remark. This is Matt. xxv. 41, "Depart from me, accursed, into the eternal fire, which is prepared for the devil and his angels." This is quoted by Justin as follows: "Go ye into the outer darkness, which the Father prepared for Satan and his angels." (*Dial.* c. 76.) The Clementine Homilies (xix. 2) agrees with Justin, except that it reads "the devil" for "Satan."

Let us examine the variations from the text of Matthew, and see whether they justify the conclusion that the quotations were taken from a different Gospel.

The first is the substitution of ὑπάγετε, which I have rendered "Go ye," for πορεύεσθε, translated in the common version "depart." The two words, however, differ much less, as they are used in Greek, than *go* and *depart* in English. The common rendering of both is "go." We have here merely the substitution of one synonymous word for another, which is very frequent in quotations from memory. Tischendorf cites for the reading ὑπάγετε here the Sinaitic MS. and HIPPOLYTUS (*De Antichr.* c. 65); so ORIGEN on Rom. xiii. 38 in Cramer's *Catena* (p.156) referred to in the *Addenda* to Tregelles's Greek Test.; to which may be added DIDYMUS (*Adv. Manich.* c. 13, Migne xxxix. 1104), ASTERIUS (*Orat.* ii. *in Ps.* v., Migne xl. 412), THEODORET (*In Ps.* lxi. 13, M. lxxx. 1336), and BASIL OF SELEUCIA (*Orat.* xl. § 2, M. lxxxv. 461). Chrysostom in quoting the passage substitutes ἀπέλθετε for πορεύεσθε eight times (*Opp.* i. 27^b ed. Montf.; 285^e; v. 256^e; xi. 29^e; 674^t; 695^d; xii. 291^b; 727^e); and so Epiphanius once (*Hær.* lxvi. 80, p. 700), and Pseudo-Cæsarius (*Dial.* iii. *resp.* 140, Migne xxxviii. 1061). In the Latin Fathers we find *discedite*, *ite*, *abite*, and *recedite*.

---

*See, for the former, Note A; for the latter, p. 29 ff.

†The two cases are (*a*) Matt. xix. 16–18 (par. Mark x. 17 ff.; Luke xviii. 18 ff.) compared with Justin, *Dial.* c. 101, and *Apol.* i. 16, and Clem. Hom. xviii. 1, 3 (comp. iii. 57; xvii. 4). Here Justin's two quotations differ widely from each other, and neither agrees closely with the Clementines. (*b*) Matt. v. 34, 37, compared with Justin, *Apol.* i. 16; Clem. Hom. iii. 55; xix. 2; also James v. 12, where see Tischendorf's note. Here the variation is natural, of slight importance, and paralleled in Clement of Alexandria and Epiphanius. On (*a*) see Semisch, p. 371 ff.; Hilgenfeld, p. 220 ff.; Westcott, *Canon*, p. 153 f.; on (*b*) Semisch, p. 375 f.; Hilgenfeld, p. 175 f.; Westcott, p. 152 f.; Sanday, p. 122 f.

The second variation consists in the omission of ἀπ' ἐμοῦ, "from me," and (οἱ) κατηραμένοι, "(ye) accursed." This is of no account whatever, being a natural abridgment of the quotation, and very common in the citations of the passage by the Fathers; Chrysostom, for example, omits the "from me" fifteen times, the "accursed" thirteen times, and both together ten times (*Opp.* i. 103ᵈ; v. 191ᶜ; 473ᵈ; vii. 296ᵃ; 571ᵈ; viii. 356ᵈ; ix. 679ᵃ; 709ᶜ; x. 138ᵇ). The omission is still more frequent in the very numerous quotations of Augustine.

The third and most remarkable variation is the substitution of τὸ σκότος τὸ ἐξώτερον, "the outer darkness," or "the darkness without," for τὸ πῦρ τὸ αἰώνιον, "the eternal fire." The critical editors give no various reading here in addition to the quotations of Justin and the Clementines, except that of the cursive MS. No. 40 (collated by Wetstein), which has, as first written, τὸ πῦρ τὸ ἐξώτερον, "the *outer* fire," for "the *eternal* fire." It has not been observed, I believe, that this singular reading appears in a quotation of the passage by Chrysostom (*Ad Theodor. lapsum,* i. 9), according to the text of Morel's edition, supported by at least two MSS. (See Montfaucon's note in his edition of Chrysost. *Opp.* i. 11.) This, as the more difficult reading, may be the true one, though Savile and Montfaucon adopt instead αἰώνιον, "eternal," on the authority of four MSS.* But it does not appear to have been noticed that CHRYSOSTOM in two quotations of this passage substitutes the "outer darkness" for "the eternal fire." So *De Virg.* c. 24, Opp. i. 285 (349)ᵉ, ἀπέλθετε γάρ, φησίν, ἀπ' ἐμοῦ εἰς τὸ σκότος τὸ ἐξώτερον τὸ ἡτοιμασμένον κ. τ. λ. Again, *De Pœnit.* vii. 6, Opp. ii. 339 (399)ᵇ, πορεύεσθε, οἱ κατηραμένοι, εἰς τὸ σκότος τὸ ἐξώτερον κ. τ. λ. We find the same reading in BASIL THE GREAT, *Hom. in Luc.* xii. 18, Opp. ii. 50 (70)ᵈ; in THEODORE OF MOPSUESTIA in a Syriac translation (*Fragmenta Syriaca,* ed. E. Sachau, Lips. 1869, p. 12, or p. 19 of the Syriac), "discedite a me in *tenebras exteriores* quæ paratæ sunt diabolo ejusque angelis"; in THEODORET (*In Ps.* lxi. 13, Migne lxxx. 1336), who quotes the passage in connection with vv. 32-34 as follows: "Go ye (ὑπάγετε) into the *outer darkness,* where is the loud crying and gnashing of teeth"; † in BASIL OF SELEUCIA substantially (*Orat.* xl. § 2, M. lxxxv. 461), ὑπάγετε εἰς τὸ σκότος τὸ ἔ ξ ω, τὸ ἡτοιμασμένον κ. τ. λ., and in "SIMEON CIONITA," *i.e.* Symeon Stylites the younger (*Serm.* xxi. c. 2, in Mai's *Nova Patrum Biblioth.* tom. viii. (1871), pars iii. p. 104), "Depart, ye accursed, into the *outer darkness;* there shall be the wailing and gnashing of teeth."‡ Compare SULPICIUS SEVERUS, *Epist.* i. *ad Sororem,* c. 7: "Ite in *tenebras exteriores,* ubi erit fletus et stridor dentium" (Migne xx. 227ᵃ). See also Antonius Magnus, Abbas, *Epist.* xx. (Migne, *Patrol. Gr.* xl. 1058), "Recedite a me, maledicti, in ignem æternum, ubi est fletus et stridor dentium."

The use of the expression "the outer darkness" in Matt. viii. 12, xxii. 13, and especially xxv. 30, in connection with "the wailing and gnashing of teeth," and the combination of the latter also with "the furnace of fire" in Matt. xiii. 42, 50, would naturally lead to such a confusion and intermixture of different passages in quoting from memory, or quoting freely, as we see in these

---

* Since the above was written, I have noticed this reading in Philippus Solitarius, *Dioptra Rei Christianæ,* iv. 20 (Migne, *Patrol. Gr.* cxxvii. 875, b c): "Abite a me procul, longe, maledicti, *in ignem exteriorem,* qui præparatus est diabolo et angelis ejus."

† The last clause reads ὅπου ὁ βρυγμὸς καὶ ὁ ὀλολυγμὸς τῶν ὀδόντων, but the words βρυγμός and ὀλολυγμός seem to have been transposed through the mistake of a scribe.

‡ Simeon Cionita uses the expression τὸ ἐξώτερον πῦρ, "the outer fire," *Serm.* xxi. c. 1.

examples. Semisch quotes a passage from Clement of Alexandria (*Quis dives*, etc., c. 13, p. 942), in which Jesus is represented as threatening "fire *and the outer darkness*" to those who should not feed the hungry, etc. Cyril of Alexandria associates the two thus: "What *darkness* shall fall upon them ... when he shall say, Depart from me, ye accursed, into *the eternal fire*," etc. (*Hom. div.* Opp. v. pars ii. b, p. 408 f.) The fire was conceived of as burning without light. In the case of Justin there was a particular reason for the confusion of the "fire" and the "outer darkness" from the fact that he had just before quoted Matt. viii. 12, as well as the fact that "the outer darkness" is mentioned likewise in the same chapter of Matthew (xxv. 30) from which his quotation is derived (*Dial.* c. 76).

Justin's substitution of "Satan" for "the devil" is obviously unimportant. It occurs in the Jerusalem Syriac and Æthiopic versions, and was natural in the dialogue with Trypho the *Jew*.

The remaining coincidence between Justin and the Clementines in their variation from Matthew consists in the substitution of ὁ ἡτοίμασεν ὁ πατήρ, "which *the Father* prepared" (comp. ver. 34), for τὸ ἡτοιμασμένον, "which is [*or* hath been] prepared." This is of no weight, as it is merely an early various reading which Justin doubtless found in his text of Matthew. It still appears, usually as "*my* Father" for "*the* Father," in important ancient authorities, as the *Codex Bezæ* (D), the valuable cursives 1. and 22., the principal MSS. of the Old Latin version or versions (second century), in IRENÆUS four or five times ("pater," *Hær.* ii. 7. § 3; "pater meus," iii. 23. § 3; iv. 33. § 11; 40. § 2; v. 27. § 1, allus.), ORIGEN in an old Latin version four times (*Opp.* i. 87[b], allus.; ii. 177[f]; 298[d]; iii. 885[e]), CYPRIAN three times, JUVENCUS, HILARY three times, GAUDENTIUS once, AUGUSTINE, LEO MAGNUS, and the author of *De Promissis*,— for the references to these, see Sabatier; also in PHILASTRIUS (*Hær.* 114), SULPICIUS SEVERUS (*Ep.* ii. *ad Sororem*, c. 7, Migne xx. 231c), FASTIDIUS (*De Vit. Chr.* cc. 10, 13, M. l. 393, 399), EVAGRIUS presbyter (*Consult.* etc. iii. 9, M. xx. 1164), SALVIAN (*Adv. Avar.* ii. 11; x. 4; M. liii. 201, 251), and other Latin Fathers — but the reader shall be spared.— Clement of Alexandria in an allusion to this passage (*Cohort.* c. 9, p. 69) has "which the *Lord* prepared"; Origen (*Lat.*) reads six times "which *God* prepared" (*Opp.* ii. 161[e]; 346[a]; 416[f]; 431[d]; 466[b]; and iv. b. p. 48[a], ap. Pamphili *Apol.*); and we find the same reading in Tertullian, Gaudentius, Jerome (*In Isa.* l. 11), and Paulinus Nolanus. Alcimus Avitus has *Deus Pater*.— Hippolytus (*De Antichr.* c. 65) *adds* "which *my Father* prepared" to the ordinary text.

It is clear, I think, from the facts which have been presented, that there is no ground for the conclusion that Justin has here quoted an apocryphal Gospel. His variations from the common text of Matthew are easily explained, and we find them all in the quotations of the later Christian Fathers.

In the exhibition of the various readings of this passage, I have ventured to go a little beyond what was absolutely necessary for my immediate purpose, partly because the critical editions of the Greek Testament represent the patristic authorities so incompletely, but principally because it seemed desirable to expose still more fully the false assumption of *Supernatural Religion* and other writers in their reasoning about the quotations of Justin.

But to return to our main topic. We have seen that there is no *direct* evidence of any weight that Justin used either the "Gospel according to the Hebrews" (so far as this was distinguished from the Gospel according to Matthew) or the "Gospel according to Peter." That he should have taken either of these as the source of his quotations, or that either of these constituted the "Memoirs" read generally in public worship in the Christian churches of his time, is in the highest degree improbable. The "Gospel according to the Hebrews" was the Gospel exclusively used by the Ebionites or Jewish Christians; and neither Justin nor the majority of Christians in his time were Ebionites. The "Gospel according to Peter" favored the opinions of the Docetæ; but neither Justin nor the generality of Christians were Docetists. Still less can be said in behalf of the hypothesis that any other apocryphal "Gospel" of which we know anything constituted the "Memoirs" which he cites, if they were one book, or was included among them, if they were several. We must, then, either admit that Justin's "Memoirs" were our four Gospels, a supposition which, I believe, fully explains all the phenomena, or resort to Thoma's hypothesis of an "X-Gospel," *i.e.*, a Gospel of which we know nothing. The only conditions which this "X-Gospel" will then have to fulfil will be: It must have contained an account of the life and teaching of Christ which Justin and the Christians of his time believed to have been "composed by the Apostles and their companions"; it must have been received accordingly as a sacred book, of the highest authority, read in churches on the Lord's day with the writings of the Old Testament prophets; and, almost immediately after he wrote, it must have mysteriously disappeared and fallen into oblivion, leaving no trace behind.*

---

*Compare Norton, *Genuineness of the Gospels*, 1st ed. (1837), vol. i. pp. 225-230; 2d ed., i. 231 f.

www.ingramcontent.com/pod-product-compliance
Lightning Source LLC
Chambersburg PA
CBHW070514090426
42735CB00012B/2777